First Free Congregational Church

# Manual of the First Free Congregational Church of Lockport, N. Y

1885

First Free Congregational Church

**Manual of the First Free Congregational Church of Lockport, N. Y**
*1885*

ISBN/EAN: 9783337261177

Printed in Europe, USA, Canada, Australia, Japan

Cover: Foto ©Lupo / pixelio.de

More available books at **www.hansebooks.com**

OF THE

# First Free Congregational Church

OF

LOCKPORT, N. Y.

1885

LOCKPORT, N. Y.
JOURNAL BOOK AND JOB PRINTING HOUSE, 91 MAIN STREET.
1885.

# PRINCIPLES

AND

# Usages of Congregationalism.

A Christian church is a body of Christian believers, formally organized and worshipping together. In the New Testament the word "church" is always used with reference either to the general company of the redeemed, which is *the* church, or to an association of believers in some particular town or city, which is *a* church. The word never occurs in the Bible in the sense of an external, centralized organization, embracing and ruling a number of associated congregations. (See Eph. 1 : 22; 5 : 23–32. Acts 8 : 1; 9 : 31. Gal. 1 : 22. I. Cor. 1 : 2; II. Cor. 8 : 18-19.)

Congregational churches recognize but two permanent and divinely-instituted orders among church officers — pastors and deacons. The office of pastor (or shepherd) has a variety of designations in the New Testament, and is the same as bishop (or overseer) and presbyter (or elder). That these terms are used interchangeably to describe the same office may be seen by

(3)

comparing Acts 20 : 17-18 ; Tit. 1 : 5-7 : I. Pet. 5 : 1-5.
The office and duties of deacons (or servants) are clearly
set forth in Acts 6 : "Glorious humility of the Christian
church, which knows no higher titles than those of
'servant,' 'elderly-man,' 'over-looker'"!

The term "Congregational" is applied to our churches
because in them *all ecclesiastical power resides in the
congregated body of believers or members of the church*,
and not in the officers of the church, nor in ecclesiastical
bodies distinct from, or above, the church. The power
belonging to the church is, of course, purely ecclesiastical. The principal powers exercised are : 1st. The
power of electing its own officers. 2d. The power of
admitting to or excluding from its own membership.
3d. The power of forming its own confession of faith.
4th. The power of regulating the details of its own worship. 5th. The power of exercising discipline on its own
members. (See Acts i. : 15, 23-26 ; vi. : 1, 2, 3, 5 ; xv. : 2-4,
22, 23, 30 ; Mat. xviii. : 17 ; I. Cor. v. : 4, 5 ; II. Cor. ii. :
16.) In the exercise of these powers a Congregational
church is independent of all external authority. It holds
its charter of life from the Lord Jesus Christ and is ac-
countable to him alone for the manner in which it fulfills
its solemn trust. We read of no ecclesiastical body in
the New Testament, exalted above the local church and
placed between it and its divine Head, to exercise judi-
cial authority upon it. (See Mark x. : 42-44.) At the
same time churches of Christ are to come into *fellow-*

*ship* with each other, and are to live in close fraternal union, mutually giving and receiving that recognition, encouragement, sympathy, advice and admonition which the law of Christ demands. And all this is to be the result of mutual confidence and affection, not of enforced obedience to superior power. The Congregational church, therefore, that adopts a creed or persists in a course of action radically opposed to the belief and practice of the other churches, must expect to surrender its claim to their confidence and approval.

It may be disfellowshipped; but it cannot even then be coerced. If such a church still believes itself to be acting in obedience to the teachings of God's word it may claim to be a church, though it has lost its standing as a Congregational church.

Gibbon describes the early Christian churches in the cities of the old Roman Empire as being thus " united only by the ties of faith and charity." " Independence and equality," he says, " form the basis of their internal constitution." This was but the extension of the spirit and practice of the churches in New Testament times, and we believe that this establishes a sufficient basis for union among churches now.

The practical working of this theory may be seen in the Congregational churches of New England and in other parts of our land. For harmony of faith in all the essentials of evangelical religion, for purity of discipline, for Christian activity and missionary zeal, while our churches fall far below the standard of the Gospel, they do, nevertheless, compare favorably with bodies of Christians organized under other forms of government. In so far as we lack, therefore, the fault must be in ourselves; it cannot be charged to our polity. The methods by which Congregational churches come into fellowship with each other are various; conspicuous among them, however, is the use of councils, conferences and associations.

An *Ecclesiastical Council* is an advisory body, called into existence by the "letters-missive" of the church desiring its assistance. Such a church invites other churches to be present at a certain time and place by pastor and delegate to advise on certain matters mentioned in the letter-missive. When the business on hand is transacted and its advice or assistance is given the council adjourns *sine die*. Councils are most frequently called for advice with regard to the organization and recognition of churches, the ordination and installation of pastors or their dismissal, and the administration of discipline.

Any church, however, that desires the advice of the churches in any other matter may call a council to their aid. When there is division in a church and the two parties are unable to unite in calling a mutual council, either party is at liberty to invite an *ex parte* council.

*Associations* are societies of ordained ministers, formed especially for ministerial improvement and usefulness.

The pastor of this church is a member of the "Ontario Assocation."

*Conferences* are assemblies of neighboring churches for mutual conference and co-operation. Each church within certain prescribed limits is entitled to representation by pastor and delegates. Every conference has its stated meetings. This church is connected with the "Ontario Conference," which holds its meetings annually in the month of December.

The *General Association* is a union of all the local conferences and associations in a particular state. When the churches in the state are numerous, as in New England, it is composed of delegates appointed by these local bodies. But when the churches are fewer in number, as in this state, it embraces all the members of the local ministerial associations, together with one delegate from each Congregational church in the state. This body meets annually and hears reports, and suggests advice on all matters connected with the spiritual prosperity of the churches, their mutual relations and their general work of benevolence and evangelization.

The meeting of the General Association of the state of New York with this church in October, 1876, will be remembered in this connection.

The *National Council* is the latest development of organized Congregationalism. It meets triennially and is composed of delegates from the local bodies. It does on a national scale what the General Associations are doing in their several states.

It will be particularly noticed that all these bodies are simply *advisory*, and that none of them possess any ecclesiastical authority. Another bond of union between our churches is our great *benevolent societies*. These are organizations working in different directions toward the evangelization of our country and of the world. They are as follows: "The American Board of Commissioners for Foreign Missions," "The American Home Missionary Society," "The American Missionary Association" (where the work is among the foreign races in this country, African, Indian and Chinese), "The American Congregational Union" (which assists weak churches in building houses of worship), "The American College and Education Society," "The Congregational Sunday School and Publishing Society," "The New West Educational Commission" and "The Ministerial Relief Fund of the Congregational Churches." These are dependent for the prosecution of their work upon the voluntary offerings of Congregational churches.

They are the almoners of our gifts, and by them the churches are accomplishing grand results, which, without them, it would be impossible to attain. Thus the independence of Congregational churches is neither discord nor isolation. On the contrary, they live in close fraternal union ; they ask and receive advice and assistance from each other, often admonishing one another as brethren, and the more than three thousand Congregational churches of this land unite voluntarily together in carrying forward a general scheme of missionary operations in which considerably over one million dollars is expended annually. But in all this only *fellowship* on the basis of *equality* is recognized. No Congregational church admits any authority superior to itself, save the one Lord and Master Jesus Christ, who has revealed himself in His Holy Word, and who, by His Spirit, is constantly present in the church to sanctify and guide.

Though preferring these principles of organization, on what are known to be scriptural grounds, and grounds of wisdom and expediency, Congregational churches do not fail to recognize with fraternal fellowship all societies of believers, who love our Lord Jesus Christ in sincerity, as Christian churches, and to esteem them very highly for their works' sake. As Congregationalists, we have an open communion; we give letters to our own members to join churches of other evangelical denominations, and receive members on such letters from them; and we seek to co-operate heartily with Christians of whatever name in endeavors to promote the common cause of our divine Redeemer.

### DIFFERENCES FROM OTHER DENOMINATIONS.

Congregationalists differ from Presbyterians principally in church-government. Presbyterian churches have each a body of lay elders, who, with their pastor, compose the session by whom the government of the church is exercised, members being received or excluded by their vote alone, who also keep the church records and make their report to the presbytery, which approves or condemns. The presbytery has power to control the session and reverse their proceedings. Over the presbytery is the synod, composed of several presbyteries, and above the synod is the general assembly, formed by delegates from all the presbyteries in the land. These delegates are appointed by the presbyteries, and are always ministers or elders. A case of discipline may be carried up successively through all the judications to the general assembly. The people have no voice in the system except when the elders are first elected.

Congregationalists differ from Baptists with regard to baptism and church communion. Baptists hold that immersion alone is baptism; that none but adult believers should be baptized, and that none but immersed professors should be admitted to the Lord's table, while Congregationalists admit the validity of any baptism in which water is applied to the person in the name of the Trinity, and believe that baptism should also be given to the infant children of believers, and welcome to the Lord's table all evangelical Christians.

Congregationalists differ from Methodists chiefly in church government, the latter governing their churches by bishops and conferences, who legislate for the whole body and appoint and remove ministers.

Congregationalists differ from Episcopalians in cere-

monies of worship and in church government. The
Episcopalians hold to three orders in the ministry, and
confide the admission and exclusion of members to the
pastor and the diocesan bishop, who is set over the
churches and ministers of a particular district, and
alone has power to confirm members and ord· in ministers. Among Congregationalists every· pastor is a
bishop, as among the New Testament churches, and all
ministers are equal in office.

## INTERCOURSE WITH OTHER DENOMINATIONS.

Congregationalism, desiring to be free from any nar-
row sectarianism, insists upon no denominational pecu-
liarities as the condition of fellowship. This principle is
carried out in intercourse with other denominations. At
their seasons of communion, Congregational churches
invite all church-members, who are in regular standing
in *any evangelical denomination*, and who are honoring
their profession by a godly life, to sit down with them at
the table of the Lord. If any of their members wish
to unite with churches of other evangelical denominations letters are given to such churches; or if any come
from such denominations and there is no evidence against
their Christian character, they are received as from sis-
ter churches.

The principles of the Congregational polity are thus
seen to be accordant with the Scriptures, and with the
practice of the first and apostolic ages of Christianity.

A commission of twenty-two ministers, appointed under the direction of the National Council of the Congregational churches of the United States, to " prepare a simple and comprehensive exposition of the truths of the glorious gospel of the blessed God for the instruction and edification of the churches," reported December 19, 1883, and as a brief exposition of the creed of Congregational churches, there is here given the

## STATEMENT OF DOCTRINE.

1. We believe in one God, the Father Almighty, Maker of heaven and earth, and of all things, visible and invisible ;

And in Jesus Christ, his only Son, our Lord, who is of one substance with the Father, by whom all things were made ;

And in the Holy Spirit, the Lord and Giver of Life, who is sent from the Father and Son, and who, together with the Father and Son, is worshiped and glorified.

2. We believe that the providence of God, by which he executes his eternal purposes in the government of the world, is in and over all events ; yet so that the freedom and responsibility of man are not impaired, and sin is the act of the creature alone.

3. We believe that man was made in the image of God, that he might know, love and obey God, and enjoy him forever ; that our first parents, by disobedience, fell under the righteous condemnation of God ; and that all

men are so alienated from God that there is no salvation from the guilt and power of sin, except through God's redeeming grace.

4. We believe that God would have all men return to him; that to this end he has made himself known, not only through the works of nature, the course of his providence, and the consciences of men, but also through supernatural revelations made especially to a chosen people, and above all, when the fulness of time was come, through Jesus Christ, His Son.

5. We believe that the Scriptures of the Old and New Testaments are the record of God's revelation of himself in the work of redemption; that they were written by men under the especial guidance of the Holy Spirit; that they are able to make wise unto salvation; and that they constitute the authoritative standard by which religious teaching and human conduct are to be judged.

6. We believe that the love of God to sinful men has found its highest expression in the redemptive work of His Son, who became man, uniting his divine nature with our human nature in one person; who was tempted like other men, yet without sin; who, by his humiliation, his holy obedience, his sufferings, his death on the cross and his resurrection, became a perfect Redeemer, whose sacrifice of himself for the sins of the world declares the righteousness of God, and is the sole and sufficient ground of forgiveness and of reconciliation with him.

7. We believe that Jesus Christ, after he nad risen from the dead, ascended into heaven, where, as the one mediator between God and man, he carries forward his work of saving men; that he sends the Holy Spirit to convict them of sin, and to lead them to repentance and faith; and that those who, through renewing grace, turn to righteousness and trust in Jesus Christ as their Redeemer, receive for his sake the forgiveness of their sins, and are made the children of God.

8. We believe that those who are thus regenerated and justified, grow in sanctified character through fellowship with Christ, the indwelling of the Holy Spirit, and obedience to the truth; that a holy life is the fruit and evidence of saving faith, and that the believer's hope of continuance in such a life is in the preserving grace of God.

9. We believe that Jesus Christ came to establish among men the kingdom of God, the reign of truth and love, righteousness and peace; that to Jesus Christ, the head of this kingdom, Christians are directly responsible in faith and conduct, and that to him all have immediate access without mediatorial or priestly intervention.

10. We believe that the Church of Christ, invisible and spiritual, comprises all true believers, whose duty it is to associate themselves in churches, for the maintenance of worship, for the promotion of spiritual growth and fellowship, and for the conversion of men; that

these churches, under the guidance of the Holy Scriptures and in fellowship with one another, may determine—each for itself—their organization, statements of belief and forms of worship ; may appoint and set apart their own ministers, and should co-operate in the work which Christ has committed to them for the furtherance of the Gospel throughout the world.

11.   We believe in the observance of the Lord's Day, as a day of holy rest and worship ; in the ministry of the Word ; and in the two sacraments which Christ has appointed for his church ; baptism, to be administered to believers and their children, as the sign of cleansing from sin, of union to Christ, and of the impartation of the Holy Spirit ; and the Lord's Supper, as a symbol of his atoning death, a seal of its efficacy, and a means whereby he confirms and strengthens the spiritual union and communion of believers with himself.

12.   We believe in the ultimate prevalence of the kingdom of Christ over all the earth ; in the glorious appearing of the great God and our Saviour Jesus Christ ; in the resurrection of the dead, and in a final judgment, the issues of which are that the wicked shall go away into everlasting punishment, but the righteous into life eternal.

# HISTORY

OF THE

# First Free Congregational Church,

## OF LOCKPORT, N. Y.

This church was organized on Thursday, June 7th, 1838, in a hall in the Boughton Block.

The record of the proceedings reads as follows: A meeting for the purpose of constituting a " Congregational church " was called in the village of Lockport, June 7th, 1838. After a sermon by the Rev. William Bacon, of Troy, the meeting was organized by the appointment of Rev. H. G. Nott, of Buffalo, as moderator, and Oliver Parsons, as clerk.

Rev. Mr. Sherwood, of Wilson, present and assisting. Prayer by Rev. Mr. Sherwood.

A letter of dismission from the First Presbyterian church, of Lockport, was presented by Marcus Stickney and forty-three others. Alpheus Phelps also presented a letter from the Presbyterian church, of Ogden, Monroe county, whereupon it was resolved that these persons be constituted into a church to be known as " The First

Free Congregational Church of Lockport." The first article of the constitution then adopted reads as follows:

ART. 1. This church shall be called the First Free Congregational church of Lockport, and the Society connected therewith known as the "Society of the First Free Congregational Church of Lockport."

The word "free" was used to express the deep convictions which the church held in regard to the evil of slavery; and for the reason that the word condemns every form of sin, it has doubtless caused the members of the church to remember the duty of earnestly opposing other evils which threaten society.

After its formation the church worshiped for a season in what was known as the Boughton block, on Canal street, the north side and a little west of the Big Bridge. From thence they moved into the hall in the Moyer block, now occupied by the "Grand Army of the Republic."

The first meeting-house was dedicated on Thursday, July 23d, 1840, occupying the site of the present building. It was struck by lightning May 22d, 1853, when Luther Crocker was killed and some others injured. The edifice was burned November 2d, 1854, in the great fire which consumed nearly all the buildings occupying the block bounded by Transit, Main, Canal and Niagara streets.

Rev. William Bacon served the church in a ministerial capacity from its organization to August 24th,

1841. Rev. Washington Rosevelt supplied the pulpit from the dismission of William Bacon to May 1st, 1842. Rev. William F. Curry acted as minister of the church from May 1st, 1842, to August 6th, 1844.

Rev. Edgar Perkins commenced his ministerial labors with the church on the first Sabbath in December, 1844, and was ordained its pastor June 25th, 1845. He was dismissed at his own request June 3d, 1849, and Rev. Edward W. Gilman ordained his successor December 4th, 1849. Edward W. Gilman's connection with the church continued until June 17th, 1856, when it was dissolved by mutual consent. From which time the pulpit was supplied by Rev. J. D. Potter, Rev. F. W. Brauns and others, until the installation of Rev. Joseph L. Bennett, on the 15th of October, 1857. That day was made still more memorable in the history of the church by the dedication of their house of worship, built in the place of the former, which had been consumed by fire. The present structure is of stone, in the Norman style of architecture.

The pastorate of Rev. Joseph L. Bennett continued until the 12th day of January, 1871, when, at his own request, the pastoral relation was dissolved by the aid of a mutual Ecclesiastical Council, to enable him to become pastor of Plymouth Congregational church in the city of Indianapolis.

The pulpit was then supplied by different clergymen, until the 24th day of May, 1871, when Rev. James W.

Cooper was tendered a call to become pastor of the church, which he accepted, and commenced his labors June 10th, 1871, and was installed pastor on the 23d day of June, 1871.

Mr Cooper continued pastor until the 21st day of February, 1878, when, at his own request, that relation was dissolved to enable him to become pastor of the South Congregational church in the city of New Britain, in the state of Connecticut.

After the dismission of Mr. Cooper the pulpit was supplied by different clergymen until the 13th day of August, 1878, when Rev. Ezra Tinker was engaged as stated supply for one year. He supplied the pulpit until the 7th day of May, 1879, when he resigned to take charge of a new church in the city of New York.

July 10th, 1879, a call to become pastor of the church was extended to Rev. Edward B. Furbish, of Potsdam, N. Y. He accepted the call, commenced his labors with the church on the 20th day of September, 1879, and was installed pastor on the 23d day of October, 1879, which pastoral relation still continues.

# Constitution of the Church.

## I. NAME.

The name of this church shall be the "FIRST FREE CONGREGATIONAL CHURCH OF LOCKPORT, N. Y."

## II. OBJECT.

The object of this church is to unite true disciples of the Lord Jesus Christ in the observance of the ordinances of the Gospel, in the development of Christian character, and in the work of saving men.

## III. GOVERNMENT.

The government of this church is vested in the body of believers who compose it, whose majority vote is final. It is amenable to no other ecclesiastical body. It acknowledges the Lord Jesus Christ as its only Head, and receives the Scriptures as its only infallible guide in matters of faith, order and discipline.

This church, while it will control its own affairs according to its own understanding of God's Word, will yet recognize the obligation and the privilege of the communion of churches, by seeking and extending that fellowship and sympathy, advice and co-operation which the law of Christ demands.

## IV. ORDINANCES.

The Sabbath services of this church shall ordinarily be as follows: Public worship and the preaching of the Gospel at $10\frac{1}{2}$ A. M. and at 7 or $7\frac{1}{2}$ P. M. Sabbath-school at noon. Prayer-meeting at 6 or $6\frac{1}{2}$ P. M. The regular weekly meeting for conference and prayer shall be held on Wednesday evenings. Extra services as occasion requires.

The Feast of the Lord's Supper will be observed in this church ordinarily on the first Sabbath in January, March, May, July, September and November. The preparatory service will be held on the Friday evening preceding each communion Sabbath. To this communion feast the church invites all who love our Lord Jesus Christ in sincerity and are living a life of faith in him.

Special services for the baptism of children may be held at least twice in each year on Sabbath afternoons. Adults will be baptized on communion Sabbaths upon the confession of their faith in Christ.

## V. MEMBERSHIP.

Persons are received as members of this church either on the confession of their Christian faith or by letter from other churches. Applicants for admission will first meet the advisory committee, and, on their recommendation, their names shall be publicly propounded to the church. At the next following "preparatory service" the church may receive them by a major vote of the members present. Those who bring letters shall then become members by uniting in covenant with this church. All others shall publicly assent to the declaration of faith and the covenant, and if they have not already received the ordinance shall be baptized.

Members of this church desiring letters of dismission and recommendation to other churches, may have their request granted by the major vote of the members present at any regular meeting, and the letter shall be issued by the clerk.

Separation can be affected as follows :

1. By death.

2. By dismission to another church.

3. By withdrawal of fellowship on the part of the church. In case of breach of covenant engagements, after reasonable but ineffectual endeavors on the part of the advisory committee for the reformation of the delinquent member, fellowship may be withdrawn with the consent of the delinquent member without a trial. After the absence of a member for three years, and a neglect or refusal to answer our communications, or replying to them in a manner unsatisfactory to the church, fellowship may be withdrawn without the consent of the absent member.

In other cases after trial and conviction of the offending member, on a written charge or charges preferred against him. After the absence of a member for three years, his residence being unknown, he shall be marked on the church register "gone," and shall not be reported among the membership of the church. But whenever such member shall reappear, at his own request he may, by vote of the church, have his name again placed on the church register.

## VI. OFFICERS.

The officers of this church shall be a pastor, six deacons, a clerk and a treasurer, all of whom shall be members of the church. These officers, together with the superintendent of the Sabbath-school and the president of the Young People's Association, shall form an advisory committee.

## VII. PASTOR.

The pastor of this church shall be an ordained minister of the Gospel and a member of this church. He shall be elected by a major vote of all the members present at the meeting at which such vote shall be taken, and when so elected and ordained or installed, shall hold his office until regularly dismissed according to the usage of Congregational churches.

It shall be his duty: 1st. To preach the Gospel and administer the ordinances of the church. 2d. To watch over the church as a faithful shepherd and care for its spiritual prosperity, devoting himself also to the spiritual interests of the Sabbath-school and the whole congregation, ministering to families in affliction, and seeking by every means the edification of believers and the conversion of the impenitent. 3d. To prudently and faithfully aid in enforcing the discipline which is prescribed by the Gospel. 4th. To preside at all meetings of the church.

## VIII.  DEACONS.

At each annual meeting of this church there shall be chosen by ballot two deacons, who shall hold their office three years.  Their duties shall be :  1st. To provide the elements for the Lord's Table and assist in the distribution of the same.  2d. To seek out the poor of the church, and, as far as practicable, secure relief for them.  3d. To assist the pastor in labors for the spiritual welfare of the church and in the proper and prudent enforcement of discipline.

## IX.  CLERK.

The clerk shall be chosen by ballot at each annual meeting, and shall hold his office one year, or until his successor be elected.  He shall keep a record of the proceedings of all business meetings of the church, a register of the church members, with the date of their reception and removal, and a record of all baptisms, and shall report the statistics of the church at each annual meeting.

## X.  TREASURER.

The treasurer shall be chosen by ballot at each annual meeting, and shall hold his office one year, or until his successor be elected. He shall receive and disburse the benevolences of the church according to their direction, and the Church Incidental fund according to the direction of the advisory committee, and shall report at each annual meeting.

## XI. ADVISORY COMMITTEE.

The advisory committee shall meet regularly once every month. Special meetings may be called by the pastor or by two deacons. Their duties shall be: 1st. To examine and recommend persons who may wish to unite with this church. 2d. To inquire into and present to the church cases of discipline. 3d. To recommend to the church objects for benevolent contribution. 4th. To advise with the pastor, and have a special oversight of the interests of the church, and to do whatever business may be referred to them by the church.

## XII. BUSINESS MEETINGS.

The annual business meeting of this church shall be held on the first Wednesday in January, the church year to include the twelve months beginning January 1st. At this meeting reports shall be submitted by the deacons, the clerk, the treasurer and the superintendent of the Sabbath-school; two deacons, a clerk and a treasurer shall be elected by ballot; the benevolences of the church for the ensuing year shall be arranged; the register of membership shall be revised, and such other business transacted as may be deemed necessary.

Ordinary business, such as the receiving and dismissing of members, may be transacted at any of the regularly appointed church services. Special business meetings may be called by the pastor, or by two deacons, or by any five members, notice thereof being given at a regular church service.

The pastor shall regularly act as moderator at all church meetings. In his absence a moderator shall be chosen by a major vote.

### XIII. RIGHTS OF MEMBERS.

Every member of this church in good standing is entitled to a vote on all questions and in all matters brought before the church, and the decision of the majority shall in all cases govern.

If any member has private cause of complaint against another, he shall seek immediately to have it removed in a Christian manner, according to the rule prescribed by our Lord Jesus Christ in Matthew xviii. 15-18. Complaints intended for the action of the church shall first be presented to the advisory committee, who shall, upon sufficient cause, present the same to the church.

Immoral conduct, renunciation of the articles of faith or a violation of covenant engagements, are, in the view this church, public offenses deserving censure and discipline, and it is the duty of the advisory committee to inquire into such cases, and if their own efforts to effect a reformation be unavailing, to present them to the church for its action.

When complaints are brought before the church, the accused member shall be seasonably furnished by the clerk with a copy of the charges, in all their specifications, and be entitled to a full hearing. No member can be deprived of church privileges except by regular process.

In cases of discipline, instead of a trial of the offender before the body of the church, the church may, in its discretion, refer the trial of the charges to the advisory committee or other committee to be chosen by the church, with all the power and authority which the church possesses to hear and try the same; and when the same shall have been heard and tried, the said committee shall report the facts, with their opinion on them, to the church, which opinion shall be final and conclusive unless the church shall allow a re-examination of the case upon the facts as so found by said committee; and in the final decision of the case the church may admonish or exclude the offending member from its fellowship, or both, as the motion of the committee may require, and fellowship may be withdrawn.

## XIV. BENEVOLENCE.

The offering of gifts for missionary and charitable purposes shall be made a part of the worship of this church at each Sabbath morning service. The church, at its annual meeting, shall prepare a schedule of benevolences for the ensuing year, in which shall be designated the causes, with the amounts of percentages to be given to each; and all money contributed during the year, and not otherwise designated by the donors, shall be disbursed by the treasurer according to this schedule.

### XV. SABBATH-SCHOOL.

The officers of the Sabbath school connected with this church shall be a superintendent and an assistant superintendent, a secretary, a treasurer and librarians. The superintendent and assistant superintendent shall be elected annually, by ballot, by the school, and shall be members of this church in good standing. The other officers shall be appointed by them.

While the church thus places the government of the Sabbath-school in its own hands, it does not surrender the general oversight of its affairs, but retains the right to act directly in its management whenever such a course is thought proper.

The superintendent of the school shall present to the church at each annual meeting a report showing the number of classes and members, the attendance, the benevolent contributions, the current expenses and the general condition and prospects of the school, and this report shall be placed on file by the clerk of the church.

### XVI. INTEMPERANCE.

In view of the fact that intemperance is one of the greatest social evils of the day, threatening the moral and religious life of our community, it is the opinion of this church that the use of or the traffic in intoxicating drinks as a beverage is inconsistent with the spirit and requirements of the Christian religion, and that it is the duty of every Christian to do all in his power to rescue the tempted and save the fallen, and in every way to oppose the advance of this enormous sin.

### XVII.  AMENDMENTS.

Amendments to this constitution or changes in the form for the reception of members shall be made only by a three-fourths vote of all the members present at a meeting regularly called for that purpose.

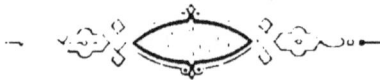

# FORM FOR THE

# Reception of Members to the Church.

---

[The names of the accepted candidates for admission to the church having been announced, the pastor shall invite them to come forward and stand near the communion table. He will then proceed as follows:]

Hear the gracious words of our Lord:

"Come unto me, all ye that labor and are heavy laden, and I will give you rest."

"Take my yoke upon you, and learn of me, for I am meek and lowly in heart, and ye shall find rest unto your souls. For my yoke is easy and my burden is light."

*Dearly Beloved:* You have come forward to confess your faith in the Lord Jesus Christ, and to pay your vows unto the Lord now in the presence of his people. With the heart man believeth unto righteousness, and with the mouth confession is made unto salvation.

You stand here at Christ's bidding; and you may venture confidently to make your covenant with him, and to confess his name before men, if you trust in his grace, with the sincere desire to be his alone.

( 30 )

Lift up your hearts then with us to the Lord, while we pray that our God may count you worthy of this calling and may fulfill all the good pleasure of his goodness and the work of faith with power. Let us pray.

(Prayer shall here be offered by the pastor.)

### CONFESSION OF FAITH.

With the whole Church of Christ in earth and heaven, we confess our faith in God, the Father, the Son, and the Holy Ghost, the Only Living and True God: in Jesus Christ, the Incarnate Word, who is exalted to be our Redeemer and King: and in the Holy Comforter, who is present in the church, to regenerate and sanctify the soul.

With the whole church, we confess the common sinfulness and ruin of our race; and we acknowledge that it is only through the work accomplished by the life and expiatory death of Christ that believers in him are justified before God, receive the remission of sins, and through the presence and grace of the Holy Comforter, are delivered from the power of sin, and perfected in holiness.

We believe, also, in the organized and visible church; in the ministry of the Word; in the sacraments of baptism and the Lord's Supper; in the resurrection of the dead and in the final judgment, the issues of which are eternal life and everlasting death.

We receive these truths on the testimony of God, given through prophets and apostles, and in the life, the

miracles, the death, and the resurrection of His Son, our
divine Redeemer — a testimony preserved for the church
in the Scriptures of the Old and New Testaments, which
were composed by holy men, as they were moved by the
Holy Ghost.

Do you accept this as the confession of your faith?
(To this question the candidate shall respond audibly, "*I do.*"

#### COVENANT WITH THE LORD.

And now humbling yourself before the Father, Son
and Holy Ghost, you do confess the sin of your unre-
generate life, and penitently renouncing the same you do
enter freely and cordially into the everlasting covenant
of grace?

You solemnly give yourselves up to God to be wholly
his; to be governed by his laws; to be guided by his
spirit; to be disposed of by his providence; to be saved
by his grace? Before God, and in the presence of these
witnesses, you avow yourselves the disciples of the Lord
Jesus Christ; and you do confess your purpose, according to the grace given unto you, to obey the truth
through the spirit unto unfeigned love of the brethren,
and to let your light so shine before men that they may
see your good works and glorify your Father which is in
heaven?

(The candidates shall respond as above.)

#### BAPTISM.

[In regard to some of you] we recognize with thank-
fulness in this your public confession of Christ, the first

of that dedication to God which was made in your early
years. The sign of consecration to the Christian life has
once been placed upon you and need not be repeated.

And those of you who were not thus baptized we welcome to this ordinance. [Or, we now welcome you to
the ordinance of baptism.] With humility and joy receive the holy rite, a visible sign of the abounding grace
of God in the remission of your sins, and of your
consecration henceforth to be followers of God as dear
children.

(FORMULA FOR BAPTISM.)—"*A. B., I baptize thee into
the name of the Father, and of the Son, and of the Holy
Ghost. Amen.*"

(Persons uniting by letter will here be called upon to rise in
their places and join with the others in giving assent to the following :)

COVENANT WITH THE CHURCH.

The members of this particular church have covenanted
together to walk with each other in charity and Christian
affection, and to do all in their power to seek its peace,
edification and purity. They have promised to attend
regularly here upon the public worship of God, the sac-
rament of the Lord's Supper and the appointed meetings
of the church for conference and prayer, and to contribute of their means for the relief of the poor and
needy of their brethren and for the maintenance of
public worship.

Do you accept and assume these same engagements

2

for yourselves until your connection with us shall be orderly dissolved ?

(The candidates giving their assent to this, the members of this church will rise.)

We then, as a church, do cordially receive you into our fellowship and communion. We welcome you in the name of Christ to a part with us in the blessings and promises of his covenant, and to a share in the duties, privileges and glories of his church. We promise to walk with you in all helpfulness and brotherly love, and to offer our prayers to the great Head of the church, that he would enable you to fulfill this solemn covenant, and finally to present you, faultless, before the presence of his glory with exceeding joy.

(The pastor shall then say to all the candidates and to the church who remain standing :)

And now, beloved, remember that ye all were without Christ, being alien from the commonwealth of Israel and strangers from the covenants of promise, having no hope and without God in the world. But now, in Christ Jesus, ye are no more strangers and foreigners, but fellow-citizens of the saints and of the household of God, and are built upon the foundation of the apostles and prophets, Jesus Christ himself being the chief corner-stone.

Wherefore, beloved, building up yourselves on your most holy faith, praying in the Holy Ghost, keep yourselves in the love of God, looking for the mercy of our Lord Jesus Christ unto eternal life. *Amen.*

# Baptism of Children.

Children may be presented for baptism by Christian parents at any communion season, or upon the third Sabbath in May or the third Sabbath in October, at 3½ o'clock in the afternoon; or when occasion requires baptism will be administered at any time in the home.

[During the reading of these or other Scriptures, or the singing of an appropriate chant or hymn. the parents will bring their children forward for baptism :]

" Go ye. therefore, and teach all nations, baptizing them in the name of the Father, and of the Son, and of the Holy Ghost."

" Then will I sprinkle clean water upon you, and ye shall be clean."

" So shall he sprinkle many nations."

" Suffer little children to come unto me, and forbid them not. for of such is the kingdom of God; and he took them up in his arms and blessed them."

" For the promise is unto you and your children."

" For this child I prayed. and the Lord hath given me my petition which I asked of him. Therefore, also, I have lent him to the Lord; as long as he liveth he shall be lent to the Lord."

" He will command his children, and his household after him : and they shall keep the way of the Lord to do justice and judgment."

*Dearly Beloved :* Beliving that the covenant which God made with Abraham for himself and his posterity

( 35 )

has not been annulled by the law, but has been confirmed by Jesus Christ, the Messenger of the Covenant to all his believing people, and recognizing in the seal of baptism divinely appointed the spiritual truth that our Saviour doth effectually work in the hearts of believers and their children, you now present this child to the Lord, acknowledging that you have given him unto the Lord ; and that you do solemnly promise to instruct him in the principles of the Gospel ; to maintain before him a life of prayer and godliness, and to endeavor, in all Christian fidelity, to bring him up in the nurture and admonition of the Lord; thus by the divine blessing fitting him for the communion and fellowship of saints in the church, on earth and in heaven.

The following are some of the reasons given in the Scriptures for infant baptism :

1st. The covenant which God made with Abraham contained the blessings of the Gospel, and the Gospel contains all the blessings of the covenant. Gal. 3 : 8 : " And the Scriptures forseeing that God would justify the heathen through faith, preached before the Gospel unto Abraham." Rom. 15 : 8 : " Now I say that Jesus Christ was a minister of the circumcision for the truth of God to confirm the promises made unto the fathers." Gal. 3 : 9 : " So they which be of faith are blessed with faithful Abraham." Gen. 17 : 7 : " And I will establish my covenant between me and thee, and thy seed after thee, in their generations, for an everlasting covenant ; to be God unto thee, and to thy seed after thee." Acts 2 : 39 : " For the promise is unto you and to your children." Gal. 3 : 14 : " That the blessing of Abraham might come on the Gentiles through Jesus Christ; that we might receive the promise of the Spirit through faith." The law does not do away with the promise contained in circumcision. Gal. 3 : 17 : " And this I say, that the covenant that was confirmed before of God in Christ, the law, which was four hundred and thirty years after, cannot disannul."

2d. The Christian parent holds the same relation to his child which Abraham held to Isaac. Rom. 4 : 11 : " And he received the sign of circumcision, a seal of the righteousness of the faith which he had yet being un-circumcised : that he might be the father of all them that believe." Gal. 4 : 28 : " Now we, brethren, as Isaac was, are the children of promise."

3d. Parents, under the Gospel as expressed in the covenant wtth Abraham, received from and dedicated to God, their infant children in faith of their acceptance with God. Gen. 18 : 19 ; Judges 13 : 12 ; 1. Samuel 1 : 11, 27, 28.

4th. The Apostles and early Christians believed in the consecration of infant children to God. Acts 21 : 20, 21.

5th. The Scriptures teach that circumcision and baptism have the same meaning. Rom. 4 : 11 : " Circumcision, a seal of the righteousness of the faith." Rom. 2 :

29 : "Circumcision is that of the heart, in the spirit, and not in the letter." Deut. 30 : 6 : "And the Lord thy God will circumcise thine heart, and the heart of thy seed, to love the Lord thy God with all thine heart, and with all thy soul, that thou mayest live." Col. 2 : 11, 12 : "In whom also ye are circumcised with the circumcision made without hands, in putting off the body of the sins of the flesh by the circumcision of Christ: Buried with him in baptism, wherein also ye are risen with him through the faith of operation of God, who hath raised him from the dead."

6th. Four-sevenths of the baptisms *mentioned* by the writers of the New Testament were household baptisms. Though many were baptized, the Apostles specify but seven : The Ethiopian eunuch, Simon Magus, Saul of Tarsus, Cornelius, Lydia, the jailor of Philippi, and Crispus. In four of the cases mentioned the families were baptized. In the cases of Saul and the Ethiopian there were no families. We do not know that Simon Magus had a family. In all the cases where mention is made of persons baptized, where we know that they had households, it is stated that they were baptized with their families. Acts 16 : 15 : "She was baptized and her household ;" 33d verse, "Was baptized, he and all his, straightway." I. Cor. 1 : 16 : Paul says, "And I baptized also the household of Stephanus."

7th. The Scriptures declare that the Christian faith of one of the parents is sufficient to authorize the seal of the covenant. I. Cor. 7 : 14 : "For the unbelieving husband is sanctified by the wife, and the unbelieving wife, is sanctified by the husband : else were your children unclean ; but now are they holy."

8th. Our Lord confirmed the promise of the covenant that the blessings of the Gospel were unto believers and their children. Luke 18 : 15 ; Mark 10 : 13, 14, 16 : "And they brought unto him also infants, that he would touch them:" "and his disciples rebuked those that brought them. But when Jesus saw it, he was much displeased, and said unto them, Suffer the little children to come unto me, and forbid them not: for of such is the kingdom of God." "And he took them up in his arms, put his hands upon them, and blessed them."

The nature of his blessing is explained by his words, "for of such is the kingdom of heaven."

# CATALOGUE

OF

## OFFICERS, TEACHERS AND SCHOLARS

OF THE

# First Free Congregational Sunday School

OF LOCKPORT, N. Y.

---

"Gather the people together, men, and women, and children, and thy stranger that is within thy gates, that they may hear, and that they may learn, and fear the Lord your God, and observe to do all the words of this law : and that their children may hear and learn to fear the Lord your God, as long as ye live in the land." Deut. 31 : 12-13.

# OFFICERS—1885.

| | |
|---|---|
| E. A. HOLT, | *Superintendent* |
| DR. F. J. BAKER, | *1st. Asst Supt* |
| P. N. HASKELL, | *2d. Asst. Supt* |
| MISS ANGIE BELDEN, | *3d Asst. Supt* |
| CHAS. STUKINS, | *Secretary* |
| GEO. P. KNIGHT, | *Asst Secy* |
| WM. N. TREVOR, | *Treasurer* |
| ARTHUR LERCH, | *Lib. Sen. Dept* |
| WALTER TIMMERMAN, | " |
| WALTER SIMMONS, | " |
| S. F. GOODING, | *Lib. Jun. Dept* |
| GARDNER RICHARDSON, | " |
| VIRGIL GRAHAM, | " |

# Members of the Sunday School.

## JUNIOR DEPARTMENT.

Mrs. L. A. Dietrick, Teacher.

Roy Watson,
Chas. Windsor,
Geo. Millener,
Ada Fisher,
Geo. Morrill,
Augusta Eberts,
Frank Creamer,
Frank Knoop,
Ernest Carey,
Rosa Ritzenthaler,
Jessie Scott,
Frankie Sadler,
Clarene Long,
John Kline,
Willard Cross,
Emma Dysinger,
Allie Haskell,
Chas. Van Stukins,
Ida Shankles,
Frank Moyer,
Howard Noble,

Geo. A. Holt,
Helena Fitts,
Carrie Fisher,
Willie Compton,
Ona Duquette,
Robbie Lerch,
Howard Moyer,
Howard Carey,
Lee Ernest Gooding,
Alexander Scott,
Lizzie Scott,
Willie Colebity,
Elmer Ticknor,
Clara Barnes,
Willie Tolhurst,
Emma Dysinger,
Kittie L. Stukins,
Minnie Knoop,
Ada Beach,
Alfred Humphrey,
May Noble,

44

Hattie Sharer,
Bertie Van Wyck,
Minnie Chapman,
Emma Jones,
George Jones,
Jos. Longtoft,
Edward Townsend.

Nellie Wilson,
Annie Chapman,
Vinnie Chapman,
Andrew Jones,
Wm. Wilson,
Guy Van Dusen,

### Miss Julia Casey, Teacher.

Jennie Smith,
Mattie Empson,
Olive Tolhurst,
Tillie Richardson,
Ella Burch,

Mamie Lerch,
Emmma Queary,
Mamie Bailey,
Anna Martin,
Mamie Dickinson.

### Mrs. Geo. S. Blair, Teacher.

Belle Huff,
Jennie Smith,
Gertie Graham,
Mabel Granville,
Alice Richardson,
Mabel West,
Ada Lambert,
Hattie Lochner,
Harry Granville,
George Prime,
Eddie Bishop,
Arthur West,

Lena Prime,
Mamie Graham,
Flora Lovell,
Lottie Bishop,
Bertha McKnight,
Jennie Fletcher,
Bessie Lambert,
Alice Albright,
Geo. Smith,
Bertie Prime,
Ford Ryan,
Elmer Wilson,

### Miss Alice Marshall, Teacher.

Strong Grant,
Bertie Moyer,
Walter Morrill,
Elton Perry,
Ernest Crosby.

Roy Flanders.
Geo. Scott,
Harry Duquette,
Wm. Millener,

45

### Miss Luella Scott, Teacher.

Morris G. Holt,
Willie B. Gooding,
Willie Fleckser,

Howard G. Fitts,
Frank Fleckser,
Jesse Olds.

### Mrs. A. S. Gooding, Teacher.

Joseph Richardson,
Louis Moody,
Herbert Wilson,
Eddie Gaylor,
Clarence Watson,

Thos Stanton,
De Forest Porter,
Roy Fisher,
Frank Gaylor,
Erle Moody.

### Miss Mary I. Allen, Teacher.

Lena Sadler,
Ada Barnes,
Edna Mapes,
Rachel Bosserman,
Edna Eastman.

Minnie Dysinger,
Alice Rose,
Eliza Cotton,
Maud Wilson,

### Mrs J. Prime, Teacher.

Mabel Saraw,
Mattie Adams,
Mary Flanders,
Jennie Klingensmith,
Carrie Wills,
Alice Pomeroy.

Mattie Ransom,
Cora Gilrie,
Laura Chapman,
Ida Klingensmith,
Lotta Button,

### Miss Libbie Stahl, Teacher.

Chester Burch,
Fred Creamer,
Clarence De Forest,
Eddie Watts,
Edward Gantt.

Robert Creamer,
Geo. De Forest,
Chas. Richardson,
Geo. Whyman,

## Miss Hattie Dickey, Teacher.

Gertrude Le Valley,
Frankie Crapsey,
Florence Barnes,
Anna Addison,
Ida Daniels.

Georgia Le Valley,
Ida Barnes,
Lotta Richardson,
Mary Pomeroy,

## Miss Mary Duquette, Teacher.

Robbie T. Furbish,
Will Dietrick,
Clarence Barnes,
Stanley Lerch.

Albert Crapsey,
Lester Dietrick,
Eugene Barnes,

## Miss Laura Moss, Teacher.

Hattie Holt,
Grace Moody,
Edith Gaylor,
Eva Repasz,
Gertie Fleckser.

Lizzie Bogardus,
Daisy Allen,
Grace Phillips,
Grace Gilrie,

## Mrs. Wm. H. O'Keefe, Teacher.

Hattie Pitchford,
Bennie Lovell,
Libbie Burns,
Edith O'Keefe,
Mabel Pomeroy.

Nellie Clark,
Libbie Thompson,
Anna Haskell,
Mertie Lovell,

## Miss May F. Reid, Teacher.

Minnie Ford,
Alice Higgins,
Alice Wilson,
Stella Garry,
Dolly Van Wyck,
Katie Ransom.

Helena Whyman,
Cora Le Valley,
Augusta Kleinline,
Nellie Wilson,
Nellie Van Wyck,

## Mrs. W. C. Compton, Teacher.

Chas. Upson,
Geo. Reid,
Robt. Allen,
Wm. Call,
Lester Millener,
Cecil Nerber,

Eddie Upson,
Walter Burch,
Bertie Cleveland
Chas. Compton,
Chas. Martin,
Robt. Gantt.

## Miss Mary Babcock, Teacher.

Carrie V. Stukins,
Virginia Fitts,
Grace Gantt,
Nellie Holbrook,
Ida Burroughs.

Alice Holt,
Agnes King,
Fannie Gantt,
Minnie Cleveland,

---

# SENIOR DEPARTMENT.

---

## Miss Jennie Price, Teacher.

Louis Merritt,
Clinton H. Furbish,
Reuben Marsh,
Louis Olds,
Chas. Mapes,
Ellsworth Richardson

Geo. Eighme,
Ernest Rose,
Jas. Mulholland,
Louis Lefler,
Frank Ritzenthaler,

## Mrs. M. A. Long, Teacher.

Harry Sadler,
Fred Specht,
Joseph Overhulser,
Geo. Windsor.

Frank Eastman,
Walter Lambert,
Austin Morrill,

### Mr. L. B. King, Teacher.

Chas. Moss,
Edward Daggett,

Louis Olds,
Chas. Brown.

### Mrs. B. C. Barnard, Teacher.

Wm. Windsor,
Albert Barnes,
Virgil Graham,
Willie Lambert,
Burt Flanders,

Jesse Le Valley,
Robbie Allen,
Howard Balliett,
Chas. Smith,
Edward Pitchford.

### Miss Jennie McRae, Teacher.

John Chappell,
Frank Gillis.
Willie Ward.

Wm. Gillis,
Fred Bogardus,

### Miss Jessie Haines, Teacher.

Edward Longloft,
Burt Le Valley,
Charlie Parley,
Wallace Thompson.

Nelson Wilson,
Fred Ford,
Burt Saraw,

### Mrs. M. M. Richardson, Teacher

Ella Gardner,
Mary Reynolds,
Mabel Graham,
Helena Gantt,
Grace Burroughs.

Grace Holbrook,
May Adkins,
Dora Mix,
Miss Bogardus,

### Dr. F J. Baker, Teacher.

Frank Spalding,
Fred Daggett,
Gustaver Brooklyn,
Fred Trankle,

Albert Pomroy,
Chas. Herring,
B. J Jackson,
Alston Graham,

Lillian Allen,
Lyda Woodward,
Anna Bogardus,
Nellie Lerch,
Bertha Rose,
Mattie Dills,
Sarah Bradley,
Helen Kelsey,
Jennie Farrington

Mrs. Hattie Pomeroy,
Miss Pomeroy,
Mrs. Dr. F. J. Baker,
Mary Moody,
Lizzie Mapes,
Sarah Dill,
Abbie Gantt,
Miss Reynolds,

### Mr. M. L. Burrell, Teacher.

Mrs. Geo. H. Moody,
Miss Sarah Crocker,
Mrs. Wm. Le Valley,
Mrs. R. A. Barnes,
Mrs. L. Holbrook,
Mrs. I. H. Babcock,
Mrs. Dr. Mix,
Mrs. Chas. Olds,
Mrs. Emory,
Mrs. Willett.

Mrs. J. A. Ward,
Mrs. N. Lerch,
Mrs S. M. Lovell,
Mrs. Ernest Barnes,
Mrs. S. F. Bailey,
Mrs. A. J. Allen,
Mrs. Norman Pomeroy,
Mrs. J. E. Lerch,
Mrs. Chas. Long,

### Mr. Wm. H. O'Keefe, Teacher.

Frank King,
Wallace Scott,
Bertie Merritt.

Frank Ransom,
Elmer Scott,

### Mr. L. A. Dietrick, Teacher.

Louis Balliett,
Harry Babcock,
Harry Compton,
Wm. O'Hara,
Chas. Standard.

Fred Babcock,
Frank Daggett,
Tom L. Ball,
Willie Lerch,

### MR. A. L. SPALDING, Teacher.

| | |
|---|---|
| Gertie Empson, | Mamie Graham |
| Grace Spalding, | May Trevor, |
| Nellie Todd, | Grace Ticknor, |
| Della Bogardus. | |

### MISS SUSIE VAN WAGONER, Teacher.

| | |
|---|---|
| Nettie Watson, | Sarah Newton, |
| Lucy Clark, | Florence Fitts, |
| Annie Cornelius. | |

### MR. M. N. HASKELL, Teacher.

| | |
|---|---|
| Grace Webster, | Maggie Hamilton, |
| Anna Clark, | Nettie Klingensmith, |
| Matie Perry, | May Hale, |
| May Merritt, | Mamie Beach, |
| Fannie Hendershot, | Nora Pomeroy, |
| Florence Sutton, | Cora Sadler, |
| Libbie Edwards, | Anna Ball, |
| Kittie Huff, | Susie Ellis, |
| Emma Smith, | Mamie Burrell. |

### MR. ROBERT GARRY, Teacher.

| | |
|---|---|
| J. E. Baker, | Hattie Parker, |
| Aggie McRae, | Mary Babcock, |
| Maggie Gunn, | Belle Murray, |
| Miss Reynolds, | Nellie Wakeman. |

### MISS LILLIE SIMMONS, Teacher.

| | |
|---|---|
| Bertie Knowles, | Allie Lawrence, |
| Harry Gardner, | Harry Osgood, |
| Wm. Martin, | Wm. Eberts, |
| Edward Olds, | Fred Dysinger, |
| Henry Ellsworth, | Geo. Knoop, |
| Burtie Newton. | |

### Miss Libbie Balliett, Teacher.

| | |
|---|---|
| Emma Eberts, | Libbie Eberts, |
| Libbie Ritzenthaler, | Minnie Ritzenthaler. |
| May Marshall, | Grace Fisher, |
| Jessie Chambers. | |

### Mrs. L. C. Cliff, Teacher.

| | |
|---|---|
| Addie Webster, | Minnie Weaver, |
| Hattie Folger, | M. Barnard. |

### Mr. A. Stewart Gooding, Teacher.

| | |
|---|---|
| Maud Watson, | Anna Mills, |
| May Pitchford, | Libbie Ebler, |
| Alice Mapes. | |

### Mr. J. A. Ward, Teacher.

| | |
|---|---|
| Nettie Duquette, | Emma Folger, |
| Emma Hibbard, | Mr. Robert Duncan, |
| Mrs. Robert Duncan. | |

### Miss Allie Crocker, Teacher.

| | |
|---|---|
| Libbie McMaster, | Agnes Baker. |
| Kittie Weaver, | Agnes Bennett, |
| Ada M. Fitts, | May Beach, |
| Fannie McRae, | Alice Haines, |
| Lizzie Adams, | Anna Welsh, |
| Carrie Welch. | Grace Fisk. |

### Mrs. L. B. King, Teacher.

| | |
|---|---|
| Mattie Sadler, | Laura Simmons, |
| Nettie Moody, | Grace Crosby, |
| May Carroll, | Rose Rumeroy. |

## MR. ALFRED HOLMES, Teacher.

A. J. Hibbard,
H. Kingsbury,
Dr. Baker, Sr.,
Mrs. P. J. Rood,
Mrs. L. Allen,
Mrs. O. E. Moody,
Mrs. I. E. Merritt,
Mrs. Martin,
Mrs. H. Tucker,
Mrs. Kiff,
Mrs. C. Haines.

W. Simmons,
John Noble,
W. J. Graham,
Mrs. Fred Cooley,
Miss Mary White,
Mrs. W. J. Graham,
Mrs. M. W. Evans,
Mrs. Creamer,
Mrs. C. E. Odell,
Mrs. Elizabeth Stukins,

## REV. E. B. FURBISH, Teacher.

Geo. H. Moody,
M. S. Burnett,
Ernest Barnes,
Albert Crapsey,
J. E. Lerch,
Geo. Jennings,
John Prime,
S. M. Lovell.
Charles E. Odell,
Geo. Clark.

N. Lerch,
C. A. Ward,
R. A. Barnes,
Geo. S. Gooding,
Geo. Tucker,
Daniel Pomeroy,
Wm. Harrington,
Robt. Scott,
Henry A. Ellis,

## MR. E. SIMMONS, Teacher.

### SUMMARY.

| | |
|---|---:|
| Membership Junior Department, | 212 |
| Membership Senior Department, | 241 |
| Officers, | 13 |
| Teachers, | 40 |
| Total membership, | 506 |

February 23, 1885.

# CONSTITUTION AND BY-LAWS

## OF

# The Woman's Missionary Society

### OF THE

## FIRST FREE CONGREGATIONAL CHURCH

### OF LOCKPORT, N. Y.

ORGANIZED MARCH 27TH, 1874.

## CONSTITUTION.

### ARTICLE I.

This society shall be called "The Woman's Missionary Society of the First Free Congregational Church of Lockport, N. Y.," auxiliary to the "Woman's Board of Missions" of Boston.

### ARTICLE II.

The officers shall be a president, vice-president, secretary, treasurer and one or more collectors, which officers, with the vice-president of Ontario Association of New York state branch, and the president of Mission Circle, shall constitute the executive committee.

### ARTICLE III.

The object of this society is to engage the earnest, systematic co-operation of Christian women in sending out and supporting female missionaries, native teachers and Bible readers to heathen women, through the agency of the "American Board of Commissioners for Foreign Missions."

### ARTICLE IV.

The money raised by this society shall be sent to the treasurer of New York state branch at Syracuse.

### ARTICLE V.

Any lady may become a member of this society by recording her name and pledging herself to make some contribution every week, payable monthly.

### ARTICLE VI.

Any person may become a life member of the "Woman's Board of Missions" by the payment of twenty-five dollars ($25 00).

### ARTICLE VII.

Any member wishing to withdraw, after giving notice of her desire shall be honorably discharged by a vote of this society.

## BY-LAWS.

SECTION 1. The regular monthly meeting of this society shall be on Friday afternoon, after the first Sunday of every month.

SEC. 2. The president shall preside at all meetings, and have a general oversight of the interests of the society.

Sec. 3. The vice-president shall take the place of the president when absent, and, in case of a vacancy of that office, perform the duties until another election.

Sec. 4. The secretary shall keep accurate minutes of the proceedings of the society, take charge of the records and papers and conduct the necessary correspondence.

Sec. 5. The treasurer shall keep the list of membership, receive and disburse money according to the vote of the society, and report the state of the treasury at each meeting.

Sec. 6. The executive committee shall call special meetings when necessary, recommend the appropriation of funds, and consult concerning the best interests of the society.

Sec. 7. The order of exercises for the regular meetings will usually be as follows :

1. Devotional exercises.
2. Minutes of last meeting read by the secretary.
3. Report of the treasurer.
4. Unfinished business.
5. New business.
6. Missionary intelligence.
7. Devotional exercises.

Sec. 8. The annual meetings of this society shall be held in September.

# PREAMBLE AND CONSTITUTION

OF

# 𝕿𝖍𝖊 𝖄𝖔𝖚𝖓𝖌 𝕻𝖊𝖔𝖕𝖑𝖊'𝖘 𝕬𝖘𝖘𝖔𝖈𝖎𝖆𝖙𝖎𝖔𝖓

OF THE

## First Free Congregational Church

OF LOCKPORT, N. Y.

---

## LIST OF OFFICERS.

| | |
|---|---|
| B. F. Jackson, - - - | *President* |
| Louis G. Merritt, - - | *Vice-President* |
| Walter L. Simmons, - - | *Secretary* |
| Miss F. Edith Baker, - | *Treasurer* |

### ADVISORY COMMITTEE.

| | | |
|---|---|---|
| S. M. Lovell, | Alice Crocker, | Laura Moss. |

### ENTERTAINMENT COMMITTEE.

| | | |
|---|---|---|
| Chas. Moss, | Geo. Eighme, | M. S. Burnette, |
| Hattie Dickey, | May Merritt, | Agnes Baker. |

### LOOKOUT COMMITTEE.

| | | |
|---|---|---|
| M. N. Haskell, | Geo. S. Blair, | Frank Spalding, |
| S. M. Lovell, | Jessie Haines, | Belle Murray, |
| May Reid, | Mrs. Lovell, | Angie Belden. |

#### DECORATING COMMITTEE.

| Geo. P. Knight, | C. H. Furbish, | L. B. King, |
| A. L. Lerch, | Cleland A. Ward, | Geo. Jennings. |

#### DEVOTIONAL COMMITTEE.

| P. N. Haskell, | E. B. Furbish, | L. A. Dietrick, |
| Mrs. Geo P. Knight, | Edith Baker, | Alice Crocker. |

#### FLORAL COMMITTEE.

| Lillian Allen, | Alice Haines, | Grace Webster, |
| Grace Holbrook, | Susie Ellis, | Matie Perry. |

#### SEWING COMMITTEE

| Lillie Simmons, | Mrs. Geo. S. Blair, | Miss J. Price, |
| Luella Scott, | Mrs. L. B. King, | Miss F. Marshall. |

## PREAMBLE.

We, the subscribers, desirous of stimulating the piety of the young people of our church to more earnest and consecrated effort in the service of our Redeemer, and to promote a more social element among all of the young people of our congregation, do hereby agree to labor together for this end, and do adopt for our guide the following

## CONSTITUTION.

### ARTICLE I.

SECTION 1. The name of this association shall be the "Young People's Association of the First Free Congregational Church of Lockport."

Sec. 2. The object of this society shall be the development of Christian character and activities in its members, and the improvement of the spiritual, intellectual and social condition of our young people, by the ways and means hereinafter designated.

## ARTICLE II.

Section. 1. The members shall consist of two classes, associate and active.

Sec. 2. Associate members. Any person of good, moral character may become an associate member of this society by signing the constitution, and will have the privilege of the society, but may be excused from taking part in the prayer-meeting. It is hoped and expected that all associate members will in time become active members, and this society will work and pray for this end.

Sec. 3. Active members shall consist of all who sincerely desire to accomplish the results above specified. They shall become members by signing their names as active members to the constitution, and thereby agreeing to live up to the requirements of the same.

## ARTICLE III.

Section 1. It shall be the duty of the associate and active members of this association to promote fraternal feeling and social intercourse among its members, to visit them in sickness, to surround them with religious influences, to interest them in the meetings of the society, and to induce them to take part in its efforts for doing good. Especial attention shall also be given to searching out young people who come among us as strangers, and to assist them in forming suitable acquaintances.

SEC. 2. Prayer-meeting. It is expected that all active members of this society will be present at every meeting unless detained by some absolute necessity, and that each one will take part, however slight, in every meeting. Once each month an experience meeting shall be held, at which roll shall be called, and the response of each active member present by rising and speaking concerning their spiritual life for the past month shall be considered a renewed expression of allegiance to Christ. It is expected if any one is obliged to be absent from the experience meeting, they will send reasons for such absence by some one who attends. If any active member is absent and fails to send excuse, the lookout committee is expected to take names of such, and in a kindly spirit ascertain the reason of such absence. If any active member of this society is absent and unexcused, or present and fails to speak for three consecutive experience meetings, such an one ceases to be an active member of this society, and their names shall be placed with the associate members.

### ARTICLE IV.

SECTION 1. The officers of this association shall be a president, a vice-president, a secretary and a treasurer, and three members of an advisory committee, who shall be elected by ballot at the annual meeting, and who, together with the chairman of the standing committee, shall constitute a board of managers; the pastor shall be *ex officio* a member of the advisory committee.

SEC. 2. The president shall preside at all the meetings of the society, call such special meetings as he may deem expedient and prepare the annual report of the society's operation.

SEC. 3. The vice-president, in the absence of the president, shall perform all the duties of the office.

SEC. 4. The secretary of the society shall keep a record of its proceedings and have charge of all documents belonging to the society.

SEC. 5. The treasurer shall take charge of all moneys of the society, keep a true and correct account of the same, be prepared to report the condition of the treasury at any regular meeting of the board of managers and to disburse the money only as denoted by the board, and make a full report at the annual meeting.

SEC. 6. The board of managers shall have the control and management of all the affairs and property of the society and make their own by-laws.

### ARTICLE V.

SECTION 1. There shall be the following standing committees of the society, which shall be appointed by the president immediately after the annual meeting:

SEC. 2. A devotional and visiting committee of at least three gentlemen and three ladies, who shall have charge of all devotional meetings, visit the sick or such as request counsel or advice.

SEC. 3. An entertainment committee of at least three members, who shall provide all social, literary or musical entertainments.

SEC. 4. An executive committee of at least three gentlemen and three ladies, who shall devise ways and means for meeting the current expenses of the society.

SEC. 5. A floral committee of at least six ladies, who shall provide flowers for the church on the Sabbath and other occasions when desired by the church or this society.

SEC. 6. A decorative committee of at least six gentlemen, whose duties it shall be (with the floral committee) to decorate or drape church or chapel when it is deemed necessary.

SEC. 7. A sewing committee of six or more ladies, who shall prepare clothing, bedding, etc., for our own poor and for home and foreign missions.

SEC. 8. A lookout committee of at least three gentlemen and three ladies, whose duty it shall be to bring new members into the society, to introduce them to the work and to the other members, and to affectionately look after any who may seem indifferent to their duties.

SEC. 9. The president shall be *ex officio* member of all standing committees.

## ARTICLE VI.

SECTION 1. There shall be a regular meeting of the society on the second Tuesday of each month, and special meetings may be called by the president at the written request of five members. In the event of the absence of the president or his inability or refusal to act, a special meeting may be called by any seven members of the society by written notices subscribed by their names.

SEC. 2. The annual meeting of the society shall be held on the second Tuesday in December of each year, at which the annual report shall be read by the secretary, and officers elected for the ensuing year, a majority of the votes cast being necessary to a choice.

SEC. 3. Nine members shall constitute a quorum at any meeting of the society when business is to be transacted.

## ARTICLE VII.

SECTION 1. All vacancies occurring in the board of managers shall be filled by the president.

SEC. 2. If by any reason the office of President shall become vacant, the same can only be filled by election at a regular meeting of the society, of which one month's notice shall have been given previously.

## ARTICLE VIII.

SEC. 1. This constitution may be amended by a two-thirds vote of any regular meeting of the society, provided notice in writing of the substance of the proposed amendment shall be given at a regular meeting at least one month previous.

---

## LIST OF MEMBERS.

| | | |
|---|---|---|
| Allen, S. Lillian | Aldrich, M. C | Allen, Mary E. |
| Allen, T. A. | Baker, T. Edith | Ball, R. H. |
| Belknap, Fred | Blair, Geo. S. | Blair, Mrs. Geo. S. |
| Bradley, Sarah A. | Brown, James C. | Belden, Miss A. G |
| Baker, S. Agnes | Bogardus, Anna M. | Beach, Mamie C |
| Bronson, Cora A. | Burnette, M. S. | Balliett, L. D. |
| Bogardus, Della | Clark, Anna | Crocker, Alice E |
| Campbell, Sarah | Campbell, Florence | Compton, Wm. C. |
| Crosby, Grace | Campbell, Curt, | Campbell, C. A. |
| Custerson, B. C. | Clark, S. Lucy | Dickey, Hattie F. |
| Daniels, Elton L. | Dietrick, L A. | Dietrick, Mrs. L. A |
| Duquette, S. Nettie | Duquette, Mary J. | Daniels, Ida |
| Dill, Nettie | Dietrick, Will A. | Dietrick, Lester A. |
| Dickinson, Hattie | Davison, A. S. | Eberts, John |
| Eighme, Geo. C. | Ellis, Susie | Ellis, H. A. |
| Folger, Emma L. | Furbish, Clinton H. | Fitts, Ada M. |
| Fitts, Florence | Furbish, Rev. E. B. | Furbish, Robert T. |
| Gooding, Geo. S. | Garry, Robert | Graham, Geo. B. |
| Gardner, Ella F. | Graham, Mabel | Gillis, W P |
| Haskell, Martin N. | Hoag, Flora A | Huff, Kate |
| Holmes, Mrs. G. A. | Haines, Jessie | Harmony, Alice C. |
| Harmony, Isabel | Humphrey, John R | Hoag, Willie R. |
| Haskell, P. N. | Haskell, Mrs. M N | Haskell, Mrs. P N |
| Holmes, Alfred | Hale, May | Holbrook, Grace |
| Hendershott, Fanny | Hamilton, Maggie | Haines, Alice E |
| Isbell, Sarah E. | Jennings, Geo. H. | Jackson, B. F. |
| King, Mrs. L. B. | King, L. B. | Knight, Geo. P. |
| Knight, Mrs. Geo. P. | Klingensmith, Nettie I. | Kelsey, Helen J. |

| | | |
|---|---|---|
| LeValley, Gertrude | Lovell, S. M. | LeValley, Jesse J. |
| Leonard, Sarah J. | Lerch, A. L. | Lovell, Mrs. S. M. |
| Lerch, Mamie E. | Lerch, Arthur L. | Moore, Alex. F. |
| Merritt, Louis G. | McElroy, E. May | McRae, Isabel |
| Meyers, Wm. L. | Moss, Laura | Moss, Charles W. |
| Marshall, Fredda | Merritt, May | Mix, Nora A |
| Moody, Nettie L. | McMaster, Libbie | O'Keefe, Wm H. |
| Perry, Matie | Price, S. J. | Penfield, Emma C. |
| Reed, May F. | Richardson, E. M. | Reynolds, May |
| Rose, Bertha | Rose, E. | Stukins, Chas. |
| Saraw, Wm. | Smith, Jennie | Simmons, Lillie |
| Stahl, Libbie J. | Spalding, Frank N. | Smith, Jennie |
| Stevens, Willie H. | Simmons, Laura | Simmons, W. L. |
| Sutton, Florence | Steele, Ebbie M. | Stevens, Birdie M. |
| Scott, Luella | VanWagoner, Susie | Welsh, George H. |
| Woodward, Elida D. | Webster, Addie J. | Weaver, Minnie E |
| Woodward, J. N. | Webster, Grace E. | Watson, Nettie. |

## CONSTITUTION AND BY-LAWS

OF

# The Woman's Home Missionary Society

OF THE

## FIRST FREE CONGREGATIONAL CHURCH

OF LOCKPORT, N. Y.

---

# CONSTITUTION.

### ARTICLE I.

This society shall be called "The Woman's Home Missionary Society of the First Free Congregational Church of Lockport, N. Y."

It shall work in unison with the sewing circle of the Y. P. A. of said church, and shall be auxiliary to "The Woman's Missionary Union" of New York state by the payment thereto of at least $5.00 per year, and sending an annual report.

### ARTICLE II.

The object of this society shall be to cultivate and diffuse a deeper missionary spirit among our church members; to meet for work which shall relieve the destitute of our own church and Sabbath-school and city, or be sent in boxes to any or all of the fields embraced in the Missionary Union; also to raise funds, which shall be applied in the same manner and for the same purpose, excepting always the annual payment to " The Woman's Missionary Union."

### ARTICLE III.

The officers of this society shall be a president, three vice-presidents, six directresses, a treasurer and a secretary. These, with the six directresses of the Y. P. A., shall constitute an executive committee, five of whom shall be a quorum to transact business.

### ARTICLE IV.

The duties of the president, vice-presidents, treasurer and secretary shall be such as commonly belong to such officers.

### ARTICLE V.

It shall be the duty of the directresses to prepare the work, etc., for weekly meetings, in connection with and under the direction of the directresses of the Y. P. S. C.

### ARTICLE VI.

Any person can become a member of this society by contributing through the mite boxes distributed by its treasurer, or by the payment annually of one dollar, if so desired.

## ARTICLE VII.

Any article of this constitution may be amended at any annual meeting of this society by a two-thirds vote of those present, due notice having been given at a previous meeting.

---

# BY-LAWS.

### ARTICLE I.

SECTION 1. The devotional and business meetings of this society shall be held six (6) times per year, on the first Thursday of alternate months, beginning in October.

### ARTICLE II.

SECTION 1. The meetings for work shall be held weekly, at the homes of the members, for such successive weeks as deemed necessary by the executive committee.

### ARTICLE III.

SECTION 1. The mite boxes distributed by this society shall be opened once a year, in connection with a social, if so decided by the executive committee, or at one of the meetings.

# The Maternal Association

ONCE A MONTH, AT 3 O'CLOCK, ON THE FRIDAY FOLLWING
THE SECOND SABBATH.

# The Employment Committee.

The following are the names of members of the Employment committee, to whom all persons desiring employment or parties desiring employes should apply, stating the kind of employment or service they desire:

W. W. TREVOR.    M. N. HASKELL.    A. L. SPALDING,
MRS. L. A. DIETRICK.    MISS LIBBIE STAHL.

# Infant Baptisms.

The following list of baptisms is somewhat imperfect, from the mislaying of the early records; but as here found is exceedingly interesting, and the hope is entertained that it will lead to a more uniform observance of one of the *privileges* of the church militant :

### 1838.

James Birney Goodrich,
Julia Frances Goodrich,
Charles Safford.
Charles Winchell.
Julia Searls Clark.

*October 28.*

Allen Perry Wentworth,
Deborah Climena Wentworth.

*December 3.*

David Niles Crumb.
Caroline Crumb.
Elizabeth. Crumb.

### 1839.—*June 30.*

Martha Rebecca Jones,
Francis Bullock.
Laura Susan Bullock,
Eliza Bullock,
Milton Bullock.

*October 26.*

Helen Elizabeth Holmes,
Frances Amanda Holmes.

### 1840.—*August 28.*

George Harrison Whitcher.

*September 10*

Elizabeth Stickney Tyler,
Frances Charlotte Tyler.

*November 5.*

Helen Venelia Phelps.

### 1841.—*April 23.*

Oliver Morris Parsons,
Lucretia Safford,
George French.
Caroline Barber.

*June 26.*

Edward Payson Belden,
Augustus Stewart Gooding.

### 1842.—*February 27.*

Hannah Amelia Crocker.
John Talmadge Gailor.
George Rinaldo Dunn.
Sterling Hadley Warner.

INFANT BAPTISMS (*Continued*).

DATE AND NAME.

DATE AND NAME.

**1842.—*June* 2.**

Minerva North Boardman,
Frances Maynard Pierce.

*September* 11.

Orville Baley Whitcher.
Caroline Rowell Bussing.
George Burrell.

*November* 29.

Charles Fessenden Parker.
Clinton Ransom Parker.
Albert Butler Parker.

**1843.—*June* 25.**

William Curry Duquet.
Frances Caroline Moss.
Orpha Eliza Crocker.

*July* 9.

William Warner Allen.

*August* 25-27.

Caroline Harrison Goodrich,
Sarah Amelia Northam.

*September* 10.

Edwin Jared Curtis.

*October* 29.

Edward Russell Gailor,
Arthur Burrell.

*December* 31.

Mary Catharine Gooding.

**1844.—*February* 23.**

Catharine Sophronia Mills,
Mary Elizabeth Martin.

*April* 7.

William Goodale Warner,
Arthur Safford.

*April* 28.

Joseph Elias Morse.
Alfred Cantine Holmes.
Ezra Alanson Wentworth,

**1844.—*April* 28.**

William Henry Wentworth,
Josephine Sherman.
William Henry Sherman.
Anna Sophronia Goodrich.

*June* 30.

William Goodrich.

**1845.—*June* 29.**

Frank Weaver Morse,
Emma Whitcher.
Sarah Iddo Allen.

*July* 27.

George Dwight Dickinson.

*August* 17.

Franklin Parsons Moss.

*September* 7.

Anna Maria Russell.

*September* 14.

Lydia Maria Wright.
Angeline Goodrich Belden,
Frances Arabella Harrington.

*September* 28.

Harriet Elizabeth Safford.
Cornelia Boardman.
Frances Elizabeth Dunn.

**1846.—*June* 26.**

Mary Emma Parsons.

*July* 5.

Ann Adelia Parker.
Edward Huntington Dickinson,
Catharine Holmes.

*October* 25.

Susanna Morgan.

*November* 1.

Robert Lafleur Crocker.

## INFANT BAPTISMS (*Continued*).

DATE AND NAME. | DATE AND NAME.

**1848.—*March* 31.**
Ann Eliza Maginnis.
*November* 5.
Calvin Luther Duquet.
Martha Harriet Moss.

**1849.—*July* 1.**
Anna Cantine Holmes.
Harriet Eliza Gooding,
Agnes Eliza Perkins,
Annetta Lucy Perkins.
Charles Norman Harrington,
Charles Garrett Smith Mills,
Lucinda Porter Phelps.
Emma Elizabeth Clapp.
*July* 29.
Gertrude Childs.
*August* 5.
John Spencer Gaylord.
Hannah Amelia Whitcher,
Alice Bertha Wright.
Charles Dwight Keep.

**1850.—*March* 3.**
Marcus Stickney Tyler,
George Tyler.
*May* 26.
Isaac Henry Cady.
Anna Elizabeth Cady.
Alice Elizabeth Crocker.
*July* 14.
James Catlin Goodrich,
Ellen Rosalie Moody.
George William Cole.
Sophia Margaret Townsend.
Joseph Andrew Bloomfield.
*October* 27.
Mary Jane Parker,
Franklin Jeremiah Evans.
Morris W. Evans.
Lucinda Evans.

**1851.—*January* 5.**
Charles Augustus Raymond,
Charles Stewart Moss.
Alice Bradley Chapman.
*April* 27.
Edward M. Moody,
Ada Lucretia Clapp.
Ellen Louisa Burrell.
Mary Goodrich Prudden.
*July* 6.
Jane McMaster.
*November* 9.
Amanda Maria Phelps.

**1852.—*March* 7.**
Owen Colton Gaylord,
Caroline Gilman.
*May* 2.
Benjamin Canby Moore,
Phebe Ann Moore.
Sarah Elizabeth Moore.
Emma Catharine Moore.
Susan Ferguson.
*July* 4.
John Fay Gooding,
Mary Isabel Kingsbury,
Wilbur Samuel Raymond.
Florence Adelle Whitcher.
Mary Lucinda Gailor,
Hazen Luertius Gailor.

**1853.—*May* 1.**
Cornelia Brown Case,
George Henry Wright.
*May* 13.
Evangeline Chapman.

**1854.—*January* 1.**
Joseph Wilkinson Duquet,
David Henry Ferguson.

INFANT BAPTISMS (*Continued*).

DATE AND NAME.     DATE AND NAME.

**1854.—*February* 26.**

Lizzie Simmons Holmes,
Luther Crocker.
Emma Joanna Holt.
Francelia Antoinette Sherman.
Fuller Shepard Sherman.

*May* 7.

George Powers Raymond,
Julia Silliman Gilman.

**1855.—*April* 27.**

Charles Mortimer Southworth.

**1856.—*March* 16.**

William Percival Belden.
Anna Papworth,
John Papworth,
Arthur Gilman.

**1857.—*November* 1.**

James McMaster.

*December* 27.

Sarah Jannet Duquet.
William James Ferguson.

**1858.—*March* 7.**

Edward Simmons Clark.

*April* 25.

Alice Bennett.

*July* 4.

Addie L. Dunton.
Edward Hubbard Prudden.
Frank Hawkins.

*May* 6.

Charles Franklin Ferguson.

**1861.—*July* 7.**

Frank Tyler Clapp.

**1862.—*May* 4.**

Flora Augusta Cady.
Mary Augusta Clapp.
Henry Miller Bennett.

**1863.—*June* 28.**

William McClellan Saraw.
Ellen Jane Margaret Chappell,

**1864.—*June* 3.**

Nellie Estelle Lerch,
Mary Frances Lerch.

**1865.—*April* 13.**

Rozetta Maria Long.

**1867.—*September* 8.**

George Stewart Gooding,
Thomas A. Gooding,
Ernestine Bowman.

*November* 3.

William Fred Dunning.

*November* 10.

Edward Candee Townsend,
Elmer Bishop Townsend,
Mary Libbie Windsor,
William Austin Windsor.
Orange Judd Raymond.

**1868.—*July* 5.**

Henry DeWitt Lerch.
Arthur Leonard Lerch.

*September* 20.

George Alfred Holmes.

*September* 27.

Alice Cantine Haines.
Walter Leet Simmons,
Anna Laura Simmons.

**1869.—*March* 28**

Hattie Grace Parker.
John Patterson Hartwell.
Mary Eugenia Hartwell.

*July* 3.

Ada Mary Fitts.
Arthur H. Lerch.

## INFANT BAPTISMS (*Continued*).

DATE AND NAME.

**1873.—*July 2*.**

William Alston Graham.
Emma Mabel Graham.
Ella Frances Gardner.
Harry Leonard Gardner.
Waldo Buckley Raymond.
George Leslie Windsor,
Louis J. Balliet.
Frank Howard Balliet,
Jerry Benjamin Long.
Virgil Miller Graham.
Ida Virginia King.
Frank Herrick King,
William Baltz Lerch,
Mary Eugenia Lerch.
Austin Blair Morrell,
James Ernest Cooper.

*November 16.*

Hattie Frances Holt.
Stanley Eugene Lerch.

**1874.—*June 28*.**

Virginia Fitts.
Alvin Calhoun Lawrence.
Elizabeth Lawrence.
Edgar Cincero Leinbach.
Mary Elizabeth Leinbach,
Mary Elizabeth Grant,
Mary Edith Trautman,
Bertram Amos Moyer.

**1875.—*June 27*.**

Willis Johnson Olds.
Edwin Nelson Olds.
Agnes Milla King.
William King Morrell.
William Bronson Gooding.
Howard Gooding Fitts.
Alice Maud Holt.
Alice Rodella Bogardus,
John Freddie Bogardus,
Carrie Elizabeth Bogardus.

DATE AND NAME.

**1876.—*September 24*.**

Minnie Almira Graham.
Lois Lavina McKee.
Carrie Stukins.

**1877.—*May 13*.**

John Charles Compton.
Charles Alfred Martin.
Jennie Addie Smith,
Mabel Anna Smith.
Mary Jane Long,
Grace Mary Holbrook.
Ella Ellen Holbrook.

*October 11.*

Maurice Gooding Holt.
Helena Fitts.
Helen Lenora Prime.
Katy Weaver Lewis,
Henry Frank Lewis.
Edward Erle Moody.

**1878.—*June 28*.**

Anna Maria Haines.

**1879.—*October 26*.**

Isaac Burling Carpenter.
Lilian Dumville.
George Adams Holt.
Kittie Louisa Stukins.
George Lester Morrell.
Karl Cady Weaver.

**1880.—*July 1*.**

Amelia Long.

*September 16.*

Lee Ernest Gooding.

**1881.—*June 19*.**

Ada Grace Adkins.
Jesse Sterling Olds.
Edith Mary Olds.
Robert Wadhams Lerch.
William Carl Compton.

## INFANT BAPTISMS (*Continued*).

DATE AND NAME.

DATE AND NAME.

**1881.—***June* 19.

John Horace Noble.
Edith May Noble.
Charles Van Zandt Stukins.

*July* 17.

Mary Grace Furbish.
Josephus Allen.
Allicia Daisy Allen.
Robert McQueen Allen.

*August* 28.

Alice Harriet Colby.

**1882.—***May* 31.

Walter Allen Lerch.
Mary Louisa Baker.

*November* 13.

George Martin,
Newton Martin Haskell.

**1883.—***May* 20.

Albert Garfield Noble,
George Alonzo Prime.
Albert Gatchel Prime,
Rollin Oliver Baker.

*March* 22.

Florence Cady Weaver.

**1883.—***September* 2.

Frank Newman Allen.

**1884.—***May* 2.

Walter Scott.

*June* 8.

Alexander Barber Scott.
George Fish Scott.
Jessie McGregor Scott.
Elizabeth Lenox Anderson Scott,
Howard Evans Long.
LeRoy Porter Fisher,
Carrie Belle Fisher.
Ada Mary Fisher.
Theodore Lewis Fisher.
Frank James Moyer.
Howard Herman Moyer.
Arnold Richardson Moyer,

*August* 3.

Libbie Scofield Noble.
Alfred James Stukins.

*October* 26.

Amy Araminta Haskell.
Charles Martin Haskell.
Henry Harmon Haskell.

*November* 16.

Ora Alice Dandler.

# Officers of the Church.

## DEACONS.

At the organization of our church, June 7th, 1838, Luther Crocker and Marcus Stickney were elected deacons for one year, and Alpheus Phelps and Joseph Maynard for two years.

Up to 1871 the church had four deacons. In 1871 and since we have had six deacons, who held office for two years up to 1877. That year and since they have held office for three years, electing two each year.

The following table shows who have held the office, the time of election and the term of service of each:

| Names. | Elected. | Term of Office. |
|---|---|---|
| Luther Crocker, | 1838 to 1861, | 23 years |
| Marcus Stickney, | 1838 to 1841, | 3 " |
| Alpheus Phelps, | 1838 to 1842, | 4 " |
| Joseph Maynard, | 1838 to 1844, | 6 " |
| Edward Henderson, | 1841 to 1853, | 12 " |
| David Mather, | 1842 to 1846, | 4 " |
| Israel Dickinson, | 1844 to 1846, | 2 " |
| Curtis Lathrop, | 1846 to 1864, | 18 " |
| Oliver Parsons, | 1846 to 1847, | 1 " |
| Prosper French, | 1847 to 1850, | 3 " |
| Thomas F. Stewart, | 1850 to 1860, | 10 " |
| Hezekiah W. Nichols, | 1853 to 1875, | 22 " |

| Names. | Elected. | Term of Office. |
|---|---|---|
| Reuben C. Belden. | 1860 to 1880, | 20 years. |
| Joseph Crocker. | 1861 to 1863, | 2 " |
| Amos Holbrook. | 1863 to 1869, | 6 " |
| George B. Townsend. | 1864 to 1874, | 10 " |
| William Glover, | 1869 to 1873. | 4 " |
| Henry Thornton. | 1841 to 1847, | 6 " |
| John B. Hartwell, | 1872 to 1876. | 4 " |
| Amos Holbrook. | 1873 to 1875. | 2 " |
| William H. O'Keefe, | 1874 to 1881, | 7 " |
| Nathaniel Lerch. | 1875 to 1880. | 5 " |
| Hiram A. Cook. | 1875 to 1877. | 2 " |
| Almon M. Graham, | 1876 to 1880. | 4 " |
| Myron L. Burrell. | 1876 to ...., | .. " |
| Stephen F. Gooding. | 1877 to 1882. | 5 " |
| Morgan Van Wagoner. | 1880 to ...., | .. " |
| William B. Gould. | 1880 to ...., | .. " |
| Daniel Crocker, | 1880 to 1883. | 3 " |
| Robert Garry, | 1881 to ...., | .. " |
| Amos Holbrook, | 1882 to 1885. | 3 " |
| Jeremiah E. Lerch. | 1883 to 1884, | 1 " |
| William H. O'Keefe. | 1884 to ...., | .. " |
| Flavius J. Baker. | 1885 to ...., | -. .. " |

### CHURCH CLERKS.

| | |
|---|---|
| Oliver Parsons, | from 1838 to 1846 |
| Alfred Holmes. | from 1846 to 1848 |
| Charles R. Parker, | from 1848 to 1850 |
| Samuel Wright. | from 1850 to 1870 |
| Alfred Holmes. | from 1870 to the present time |

### SUPERINTENDENTS OF SABBATH SCHOOL.

| | |
|---|---|
| Alfred Barrett.<br>Oliver Parsons. } | from 1838 to 1840 |
| Ira Stone, | from 1840 to 1841 |
| Alfred Holmes. | from 1841 to 1850 |

E. Adams Holt, elected in 1850 and is still serving in that capacity

# CATALOGUE OF MEMBERS

OF THE

# FIRST FREE CONGREGATIONAL CHURCH

OF

## LOCKPORT, N. Y.

—

"The Lord shall count when he writeth up the people that this man was born there."

"We, being many, are one body in Christ, and every one members one of another."

"And whether one member suffer, all the members suffer with it; or one member be honored, all the members rejoice with it. Now ye are the body of Christ, and members in particular."

# Members of the Church.

Parentheses after the names of female members enclose the names or initials of the husband; * means deceased; L, letter; C, confession; W, withdrawn; G, gone.

| NO. | RECEIVED. | NAMES OF ORIGINAL MEMBERS. | | REMOVED. |
|---|---|---|---|---|
| 1 | June 7, 1838. | L. Stickney, Marcus ... ................ | W. | May 23, 1842 |
| 2 | " | Stickney, Betsey ...................... | L. | June 29, 1842 |
| 3 | " | Tyler, Milton ........................ | L. | June 1, 1842 |
| 4 | " | Tyler, Eliza M........................ | | " |
| 5 | " | Morse, Joseph C. .................... | * | Jan. 20, 1848 |
| 6 | " | Stewart, Thomas F............ ....... | L. | April 14, 1860 |
| 7 | " | Stewart, Catharine.................... | | " |
| 8 | " | Stewart, Eliza R. (Gooding)........... | L. | July 19, 1840 |
| 9 | " | Stewart, Harriet (Judd)... ..... ...... | L. | Aug. 24, 1846 |
| 10 | " | Whitcher, Bailey H.................... | * | July 25, 1865 |
| 11 | " | Whitcher, Ordelia (Niles)............. | | .............. |
| 12 | " | Lozier, Lucy ... .......... ....... | * | Oct. 11, 1874 |
| 13 | " | Lathrop, Curtis ...................... | * | Nov. 27, 1868 |
| 14 | " | Lathrop, Roxana............. ...... | * | April 27, 1862 |
| 15 | " | Lathrop, Lucy C. (Clift) ............. | L. | March 27, 1844 |
| 16 | " | Maynard, Joseph...... ............... | L. | May 22, 1848 |
| 17 | " | Maynard, Emerson E.................. | L. | Sept. 14, 1840 |
| 18 | " | Maynard, Marcia..................... | | " |
| 19 | " | Phelps, Edmund...................... | * | Sept. 30, 1878 |
| 20 | " | Jenkins, Ann E....... ........ .... | L. | Sept. 10, 1842 |
| 21 | " | Putnam, Lucina....................... | L. | March 26, 1852 |
| 22 | " | Spalding, Laura W.(Dunn)(Southworth) | * | May 30, 1883 |
| 23 | " | Winchel, Mary....................... | L. | Oct. 8, 1838 |
| 24 | " | Clark, Abigail S...................... | L. | Sept. 18, 1839 |
| 25 | " | Crocker, Luther...................... | * | Feb. 14, 1860 |
| 26 | " | Crocker, Hannah...................... | * | May 21, 1852 |
| 27 | " | Crocker, Joseph...................... | * | March 11, 1862 |
| 28 | " | Crocker, Sarah.................. ...... | | .............. |
| 29 | " | Mather, David ....................... | L. | July 5, 1850 |
| 30 | " | Mather Nancy........................ | | " |
| 31 | " | Northam, Festus......... ........... | * | April 26, 1849 |
| 32 | " | Stone, Ira............................ | L. | March 11, 1839 |
| 33 | " | Stone, Almira.................... . | | " |
| 34 | " | Stone, Lorenzo C..................... | | " |
| 35 | " | Parsons, Oliver....................... | L. | July 29, 1846 |
| 36 | " | Parsons, Martha C.................... | | |
| 37 | " | Parsons, Harriet M. (Moss)........... | * | April 5, 1853 |
| 38 | " | Parsons, William G.................. | G. | Feb. 20, 1872 |
| 39 | " | Harwood, Mary...... ............. | * | Feb. 28, 1873 |
| 40 | " | Harwood, Lucretia (Boardman)........ | L. | Feb. 21, 1851 |

(78)

## MEMBERS OF THE CHURCH (*Continued*).

| NO. | RECEIVED. | | NAMES OF ORIGINAL MEMBERS. | | REMOVED. |
|---|---|---|---|---|---|
| 41 | June 7, 1838. | L. | Goodrich, William A................... | L. | Jan. 1, 1851 |
| 42 | " | | Goodrich, Betsey Ann....... .......... | | " " |
| 43 | " | | Goodrich, Julia A. (Simmons).......... | * | Dec. 5, 1880 |
| 44 | " | | Goodrich, Nancy C. (Newhall)......... | L. | Oct. 1, 1842 |
| 45 | " | | Phelps, Alpheus...................... | * | June 29, 1843 |

**SUBSEQUENT ADDITIONS.**

| NO. | RECEIVED. | | NAMES OF ORIGINAL MEMBERS. | | REMOVED. |
|---|---|---|---|---|---|
| 46 | June 24, 1839. | L. | Safford, Henry L....................... | L | March 30, 1853 |
| 47 | " | | Safford, Adaline... .............. ..... | * | July 29, 1841 |
| 48 | " | | Simmons, Edward ..................... | | .......... ...... |
| 49 | " | | Goodrich, Isaac C..................... | L. | Oct. 11, 1846 |
| 50 | " | | Stone, Chandler...................... | L. | Sept. 1, 1839 |
| 51 | " | | Center, Susan....................... | L. | April 18, 1843 |
| 52 | " | | Lathrop, Sophronia (Brown)........... | L. | Feb. 15, 1845 |
| 53 | " | | Morgan, Lavinia...................... | L. | Nov. 5, 1856 |
| 54 | Aug. 26, 1838 | L | Safford, Mary... ........... ..... .. | L. | March 30, 1849 |
| 55 | " | | Woodhull, Samuel ................... | W. | April 13, 1848 |
| 56 | " | | Woodhull, Mary A. ................... | L | Aug. 7, 1842 |
| 57 | " | | Parker, Charles R. ................... | | |
| 58 | " | | Belden, Reuben C..................... | * | Sept. 12, 1879 |
| 59 | " | | Belden, Mary A................. | | .......... ...... |
| 60 | " | | Goodrich, Betsey A. G................ | * | Oct. 22, 1843 |
| 61 | " | | North, Orin ................... | L. | May 7, 1848 |
| 62 | " | | North Minerva. ................... | | " |
| 63 | " | C. | Shepard, Maria...................... | L. | Oct. 8, 1838 |
| 64 | " | | Clark, Rufus S .. ................... | L. | April 23, 1839 |
| 65 | " | | Goss, Abigail (Sayre)................. | G. | Feb. 20, 1872 |
| 66 | " | | Doud, Eleanor ....................... | L. | Oct. 5, 1841 |
| 67 | " | L | Crocker, Luther, Jr................. | * | May 22, 1853 |
| 68 | " | | Adams, Jerusha B. (Southworth)....... | * | June 7, 1849 |
| 69 | " | | Mills, Amelia ........................ | * | Aug. 5, 1879 |
| 70 | " | | Homes, Frances L.................... | * | Jan. 20, 1840 |
| 71 | " | | Tyler, Harriet .................... | * | Oct. 10, 1853 |
| 72 | " | | Buchanan, Samuel.................... | * | Dec. 27, 1857 |
| 73 | " | | Buchanan, Margaret................... | * | Nov. 19, 1862 |
| 74 | " | | Freeman, Daniel A................... | L. | May 20, 1840 |
| 75 | " | | Lathrop, Miriam..................... | * | Feb. 20, 1841 |
| 76 | " | | Lewis, Orissa....................... | * | Dec. 25, 1841 |
| 77 | " | | Lewis, Lucy M. (Shoemaker).......... | W. | Oct. 25, 1850 |
| 78 | " | | Lewis, Mary E (Bowne)............... | W. | April 17, 1846 |
| 79 | Oct. 28, 1838. | C. | Tompson, William A............... | W. | Dec. 8, 1838 |
| 80 | " | | Wentworth, Ezra P .. ........... ... | * | Jan. 24, 1877 |
| 81 | " | | Wentworth, Olivia A.. .............. | * | April 2, 1852 |
| 82 | " | L. | Appleby, Mary E...................... | L. | Jan. 7, 1843 |
| 83 | Dec. 30, 1838. | L. | Dunn, David R.... ................. | * | Feb. 24, 1850 |
| 84 | " | | Maynard, Moses..................... | L. | May 22, 1843 |
| 85 | " | | Fox, Parmelia .. ................... | * | Dec. ..., 1859 |
| 86 | " | | Morse, Lydia M. W.................. | * | April 13, 1365 |
| 87 | " | | Pierce, Susan....................... | L. | Feb. 27, 1846 |
| 88 | " | | Lewis, Nancy (Bramin)............... | G. | Feb. 20, 1872 |
| 89 | " | | Doud, Eunice ................... | * | June 19, 1841 |
| 90 | " | | Doud, Vesta Ann................... | L. | Oct. 10, 1840 |
| 91 | " | | Crumb, Elizabeth................... | * | March 28, 1840 |
| 92 | " | | Doud, Loretta (Brock) ... ......... | G. | Feb. 20, 1872 |
| 93 | Feb. 24, 1839 | L. | Gailor, Cynthia................... | L. | Aug. 16, 1868 |

## MEMBERS OF THE CHURCH (*Continued*).

| NO. | RECEIVED. | | SUBSEQUENT MEMBERS | | REMOVED. |
|---|---|---|---|---|---|
| 94 | Feb. 24, 1839. | L. | Putnam, Peter............. . ....... .. | * | Sept. 24, 1848 |
| 95 | May 26, 1838. | C | Safford, Charles L.............. ...... | L. | March 30, 1849 |
| 96 | " | | Crosby, Aaron..................... | L. | Nov. 22, 1872 |
| 97 | " | | Moss, Charles S..................... | * | March 10, 1853 |
| 98 | " | | Holt, Elijah A..................... | | |
| 99 | " | | Goodrich, Charles................. | | |
| 100 | " | | Jones, Benjamin................... | G. | Feb. 20, 1872 |
| 101 | " | | Jones, Sarah....... ....... | | " |
| 102 | " | | Bullock, Mary Ann............ .. ... | L. | Sept. 1, 1839 |
| 103 | " | | Newhall, Harriet W. (Parker)........... | .. .. ....... |
| 104 | " | | Stickney, Almira...................... | L. | Oct. 20, 1839 |
| 105 | " | | Harroun, Phebe ..................... | .......... | .... |
| 106 | " | | Goodrich, Angeline (Burrell)........... | .... | ... |
| 107 | " | | Harris, Charlotte M................. | L. | Oct. 16, 1848 |
| 108 | " | | Farley, Maria L. (Tunnicliff) .......... | G. | Feb. 20, 1872 |
| 109 | " | | Parker, Portia A......... . ...... | * | Dec. 22, 1842 |
| 110 | " | | Davis, Cynthia..................... | L. | Sept. 15, 1839 |
| 111 | " | | Butler, Dinah (Johnston).............. | G. | Feb. 20, 1872 |
| 112 | " | | Fitzgerald, Catharine................. | * | Jan. 14, 1841 |
| 113 | " | | Fitzgerald, Ann Eliza................ | L. | Aug. 25, 1850 |
| 114 | " | | Clark, Elizabeth Ann................. | L. | Aug. 18, 1839 |
| 115 | " | | Lathrop, Jane...................... | * | March 31, 1858 |
| 116 | " | | Anderson, Betsey................. | L. | Sept. 5, 1840 |
| 117 | " | | Doud, Lophonzo. ................. | L. | Oct. 5, 1841 |
| 118 | " | L. | Phelps, Fidelia.................... | * | Dec. 31, 1867 |
| 119 | " | | Parkis, Angeline................... | L. | Sept. 14, 1840 |
| 120 | " | | Brunson, Noah L................... | L. | March 27, 1846 |
| 121 | " | | Brunson, Sophia..... ........... | | " |
| 122 | " | | Robbins, Harriet................. | L. | Nov. 17, 1839 |
| 123 | " | | Kent, Clarissa (Blinn)............. | ........... | |
| 124 | " | | Kent, Ermina.... ...... .... ... ... | L. | Sept. 14, 1840 |
| 125 | " | | Kent, Caroline (Herrick)............. | * | Feb. 21, 1865 |
| 126 | June 30, 1839. | C. | Steele, Seymour R................... | L. | July 5, 1843 |
| 127 | " | | Steele, Lucy C.... | | " |
| 128 | " | | May, Hannah M..... ......... | * | April 16, 1840 |
| 129 | " | | Freeman, Eunice................... | L. | May 20, 1840 |
| 130 | " | | Alvord, Wealthy G.... ........ | * | Aug. 3, 1859 |
| 131 | " | | Corbin, Mary E. (Chase)............. | G. | Feb. 20, 1872 |
| 132 | " | | Hawkes, Betsey M. (Freeman)....... | L. | Aug. 29, 1849 |
| 133 | " | | Thompson, Calista M............... | L. | Aug 29, 1842 |
| 134 | " | | Hammond, Maria A.............. | L | July 23, 1839 |
| 135 | " | | Bentley, Joseph...... ...... | L. | Sept. 20, 1840 |
| 136 | " | L. | Halleck, Ann D. (Bird)........... | L. | April 26, 1871 |
| 137 | " | | Doud, Lorenzo...................... | L. | Oct 5, 1841 |
| 138 | Aug. 25, 1839. | C. | King, Harriet B.................. | L. | Aug. 12, 1840 |
| 139 | " | | Barber, Aurilla. ......... . .... | L. | Oct. 2, 1845 |
| 140 | " | | Williams, Leonora ................. | G. | Feb. 20, 1872 |
| 141 | " | | Skinner, Alvin.................... | L. | March 2, 1840 |
| 142 | " | | Buchanan, James... ............. | L. | May 22, 1843 |
| 143 | " | | Kingsley, Esther (Alberty)...... ..... | G. | Aug. 20, 1873 |
| 144 | " | | Winchester Lucinda.... ............ | L. | May 25, 1841 |
| 145 | " | | Carpenter, Angelia... ............ | * | June 18, 1854 |
| 146 | " | | Buchanan, Abigail (Wagoner)......... | G. | Aug. 20, 1873 |
| 147 | Oct. 7, 1839. | L. | Kingsley, John C................... | L. | Nov. 11, 1840 |
| 148 | " | | Gooding, Stephen F............... | L. | July 19, 1840 |
| 149 | " | C. | Allen, Alexander.. .............. | L | Jan. 29, 1847 |
| 150 | Jan. 12, 1840. | L. | Burr, Olive.................. ... | * | June 8, 1840 |

## MEMBERS OF THE CHURCH (*Continued*).

| NO. | RECEIVED. | | SUBSEQUENT MEMBERS. | | REMOVED. |
|---|---|---|---|---|---|
| 151 | Jan. 12, 1840. | L. | Robbins, Betsey | L. | June 12, 1853 |
| 152 | " | | Robbins, Caroline | | " |
| 153 | " | | Lawrence, Lydia | L. | Oct. 31, 1841 |
| 154 | " | | Kingsley, Ann J | L. | Sept. 16, 1843 |
| 155 | " | C. | Burrell, Myron L | L. | June 11, 1871 |
| 156 | March 8, 1840. | L. | Harwood, Ezra | * | May 6, 1859 |
| 157 | " | | Worrell, Margaret | L. | June 12, 1853 |
| 158 | " | C. | Holmes, Alfred | | |
| 159 | June 28, 1840. | L. | Barnes, Sophronia | L. | Aug. 12, 1840 |
| 160 | " | | Beebe, Demmiz | L. | Feb. 27, 1867 |
| 161 | " | | Crocker, Cornelia M | L. | Feb. 12, 1842 |
| 162 | " | C. | Miles, Martha (Grout) | L. | May 23, 1852 |
| 163 | Aug. 30, 1840. | L. | French, Prosper | L. | Oct. 25, 1850 |
| 164 | " | | French, Mary | | " |
| 165 | " | | Leonard, Allen | L. | Jan 3, 1843 |
| 166 | " | | Kinney, Lydia | L. | June 2, 1847 |
| 167 | " | | Belden, Henry | * | March 10, 1853 |
| 168 | " | C. | Long, Harriet, Mrs | * | Feb. 13, 1885 |
| 169 | Oct. 25, 1840. | L. | McKinley, Margaret | L. | June 28, 1841 |
| 170 | Dec. 27, 1840. | L. | Allen, Elizabeth A | L. | Dec. 24, 1847 |
| 171 | " | C | Beebe, John | W. | July 10, 1846 |
| 172 | " | | Wright, Samuel | * | July 1, 1870 |
| 173 | " | | Townsley, Lovias D | L. | July 30, 1845 |
| 174 | " | | Tucker, Mary Ann | * | March 28, 1882 |
| 175 | " | | Beebe, Lucinda M | L | Sept. 20, 1841 |
| 176 | Feb. 29, 1841. | C. | Henderson, Edward | W. | Jan. 30, 1850 |
| 177 | " | | Childs, William H | L. | Feb 28, 1855 |
| 178 | " | | Childs, Laura A | | " |
| 179 | " | | Newhall, Daniel | * | Dec. 13, 1875 |
| 180 | " | | Newhall, Harriet | * | April 20, 1878 |
| 181 | " | | Bussing, Harvey H | * | |
| 182 | " | | Newhall, Franklin | G. | Dec. 14, 1849 |
| 183 | " | | Newhall, Frederick W | L | May 7, 1848 |
| 184 | " | | Wilson, Henry C | W. | Dec. 14, 1849 |
| 185 | " | | Wilson, Maria | L. | Oct. 1, 1854 |
| 186 | " | | Wilson, Catharine L | | " |
| 187 | " | | Bussing, Avildah F | * | Oct. 18, 1855 |
| 188 | " | | Higgins, Sarah | * | Aug. 11, 1871 |
| 189 | " | | Burrell, Mary | * | May 12, 1869 |
| 190 | " | | Tucker, Frances (Payne) | W. | Jan. 8, 1873 |
| 191 | " | | Beebe, Julia (Ellis) | W. | Sept. 27, 1850 |
| 192 | " | | Valentine, Sarah | L. | Aug. 7, 1842 |
| 193 | " | | Lathrop, Fidelia | | |
| 194 | " | | Lascelles, Margaret | G. | Dec. 9, 1844 |
| 195 | " | | Pierce, Samuel P | G. | Feb. 20, 1872 |
| 196 | " | | Duquet, Joseph | W. | Dec. 12, 1873 |
| 197 | " | | Stewart, Augustus | W. | May 10, 1846 |
| 198 | " | | Woodhull, Henry | L. | Jan. 18, 1843 |
| 199 | " | | Wilbur, Joshua | W. | April 3, 1854 |
| 200 | " | | Maker, Eliza | L. | March 26, 1855 |
| 201 | " | L. | Webber, Chloe | L. | March 20, 1843 |
| 202 | " | | Webber, Almira F | | " |
| 203 | " | | Webber, Sarah A | | " |
| 204 | " | | Webber, Martha S | | " |
| 205 | " | | Pierson, Mary Ann | L. | Dec. 27, 1841 |
| 206 | " | | Newton, Gabriella (Crosby) | L. | Nov. 22, 1872 |
| 207 | April 25, 1841. | L. | Barbour, Joseph N | L. | Oct. 30, 1841 |

4

## MEMBERS OF THE CHURCH (*Continued*).

| NO. | RECEIVED. | SUBSEQUENT MEMBERS. | | REMOVED. |
|---|---|---|---|---|
| 208 | April 25, 1841. | L. Barbour, Caroline...................... | L. | Oct. 30, 1841 |
| 209 | " | Norton, Ruby..... ............... | * | March 3, 1856 |
| 210 | June 27, 1841. | L. Gooding, Stephen F..................... | L. | May 12, 1869 |
| 211 | " | Gooding Eliza R........................ | | " |
| 212 | " | Warner, Levi B....... ............ | L. | Dec. 9, 1844 |
| 213 | " | Wright, Roswell E................... | L. | July 5, 1843 |
| 214 | " | Brown, Samuel B.................... | L. | Feb. 15, 1845 |
| 215 | " | C. Harrington, Prudence............... | * | July 6, 1872 |
| 216 | " | Harrington, Mary E. (Wright)......... | | ................... |
| 217 | " | Northam, Sarah Ann.................. | L. | March 27, 1870 |
| 218 | " | Duquet, Mary.... ..... | * | Sept. 24, 1877 |
| 219 | Sept. 12 1841. | L. Rosevelt, Jane M...................... | L. | June 24, 1842 |
| 220 | " | Parsons, Silas............. ... | L. | Oct. 2, 1848 |
| 221 | " | Parsons, Lucy....... ........... | | " |
| 222 | " | Kingsley, Calvin C.................. | L. | June 3, 1844 |
| 223 | " | C. Corbin, Phebe M...... ......... | G. | Jan. 2, 1850 |
| 224 | Nov. 7, 1841. | L. Ingersoll, Hannah................. | L. | July 13, 1842 |
| 225 | " | C. Wilder, Mary Jane.............. | * | ................... |
| 226 | " | Smithson, Letitia ................ | L. | June 19, 1843 |
| 227 | Dec. 26, 1841. | L. Gilmur, David ..................... | L. | June 24, 1842 |
| 228 | " | Gilmur, Hannah P.................. | * | |
| 229 | " | Holmes, Frances M. C...:.......... | * | June 26, 1878 |
| 230 | " | Gailor, Hazen A...................... | G. | June 6, 1869 |
| 231 | " | C. Allen, Elizabeth C. K............. | L. | Jan. 29, 1847 |
| 232 | Feb. 27, 1842. | L. Dickinson, Israel.... ................ | * | Nov. 27, 1845 |
| 233 | " | Dickinson, Polly.................... | * | May 7, 1843 |
| 234 | " | Dickinson, Israel G................. | L. | May 24, 1850 |
| 235 | " | Johnson, Horace.... ............. | L. | Jan. 3, 1849 |
| 236 | " | Johnson, Sarah ..................... | | " |
| 237 | " | Lyon, Maria ...................... | | ................... |
| 238 | " | Morse, Harriet P..................... | L. | Aug. 28, 1849 |
| 239 | " | Belden, Melissa ................... | L. | Feb. 4, 1843 |
| 240 | " | Bratt, Laura ..... ............. | L. | Nov. 14, 1843 |
| 241 | " | Hull, Aurelia...................... | L. | May 29, 1843 |
| 242 | " | Davenport, Adah (Holmes)............ | L. | Oct. 25, 1857 |
| 243 | " | C. Boardman, Edwin L................ | L. | Feb. 21, 1857 |
| 244 | " | Boardman, William F................. | L. | April 17, 1846 |
| 245 | " | Harrington, Norman S............ .... | L. | July 30, 1851 |
| 246 | " | Cole, William E..................... | L. | March 27, 1844 |
| 247 | " | Newhall, Elbridge G................. | L. | March 20, 1845 |
| 248 | " | Johnson, Mary..................... | L. | Jan 3, 1849 |
| 249 | " | Stewart, Margaret.................. | L. | Aug. 23, 1850 |
| 250 | " | Howie, Jane....................... | L. | July 12, 1843 |
| 251 | April 24, 1842. | L. Davenport, Eliza Jane (Harrington).... | L. | July 30, 1851 |
| 252 | " | C. Smith, Juliette (Swan)............... | L. | Nov. 24, 1847 |
| 253 | June 26, 1842. | C. Smith, William................... | G. | Feb. 20, 1872 |
| 254 | " | L. Hadley, Stephen ................... | L. | April 18, 1844 |
| 255 | " | Hadley, Laura...................... | | " |
| 256 | " | Hall, Chapin...................... | L. | April 28, 1843 |
| 257 | " | Hall, Lydia........................ | | " |
| 258 | Aug. 28, 1842. | L. Goodrich, William ......... ......... | * | Nov. 2, 1863 |
| 259 | " | Dudley, Theodore O................. | G. | Feb. 20, 1872 |
| 260 | " | Curry, Minerva ...................... | L. | Nov. 3, 1844 |
| 261 | " | Maynard, Angeline.................. | L. | May 22, 1843 |
| 262 | " | Hulburt, Althina...... ............. | .. | Feb. 27, 1843 |
| 263 | " | C. Steel, Margaret ................... | * | Feb. 17, 1844 |
| 264 | " | Condon, Amelia...................... | L. | Oct. 21, 1844 |

## MEMBERS OF THE CHURCH (*Continued*).

| NO. | RECEIVED. | | SUBSEQUENT ADDITIONS. | | REMOVED. | |
|---|---|---|---|---|---|---|
| 265 | Oct. 30, 1842. | L. | Parker, Elijah...................... | L. | Sept. | 28, 1849 |
| 266 | " | | Parker, Rhoda ..................... | * | Nov. | 6, 1873 |
| 267 | " | | Parker, Isaac...................... | L. | March | 30, 1853 |
| 268 | " | | Parker, Amanda .................... | | .......... | |
| 269 | " | | Parker, Cornelia (Harmony)........... | * | Aug. | 20, 1852 |
| 270 | " | C. | Warner, Jane M..................... | L. | April | 18, 1844 |
| 271 | Dec. 29, 1842. | L. | Harroun, Phebe..................... | L. | May | 7, 1843 |
| 272 | " | | Brown, John G...................... | L. | Aug. | 25, 1845 |
| 273 | " | | Brown, Lucy........................ | | " | |
| 274 | " | | Curtis, Worthy..................... | L. | Nov. | 15, 1843 |
| 275 | " | | Curtis, A.......................... | | " | |
| 276 | Feb. 26, 1843. | L. | Davenport, Darius ................. | L | June | 30, 1871 |
| 277 | " | | Davenport, Clarissa ............... | * | Jan'y | 13, 1864 |
| 278 | " | | Mott, Chloe........................ | L. | May | 3, 1846 |
| 279 | " | C. | Boardman, Henry................... | G. | Feb. | 20, 1872 |
| 280 | " | | Jewell, Graham H .................. | L. | May | 5, 1844 |
| 281 | " | | Woolcott, Anson. .... ............ | W. | July | 12. 1846 |
| 282 | " | | Newnall, Daniel, Jr................ | L. | Nov. | 3, 1844 |
| 283 | " | | Donnelly, Dudley.................. | W. | May | 24, 1850 |
| 284 | " | | Williams, Henry F................. | W. | March | 5, 1846 |
| 285 | " | | Graves, George.................... | W. | Sept. | 19, 1847 |
| 286 | " | | Dickinson, Sophia................. | L. | May | 24, 1850 |
| 287 | " | | Longley, Mary..................... | L. | June | 11, 1843 |
| 288 | " | | Boardman, Lucy I.................. | L. | May | 29, 1854 |
| 289 | " | | Safford, Rebecca (North)............. | L. | Nov. | 15, 1848 |
| 290 | " | | Harwood, Jane E. (Colton).......... .. | L. | June | 14, 1850 |
| 291 | " | | Jones, D. Ellen.................... | L | Sept. | 6, 1843 |
| 292 | " | | Payne, Sarah (Martin).. .......... | L | April | 21, 1855 |
| 293 | " | | Lathrop, Lucitta (Hawkins) ......... | * | Jan. | 30, 1858 |
| 294 | " | | Tucker, Mary Ann 2d (O'Brien)....... | * | March | 30, 1868 |
| 295 | " | | Currey, Mary Ann.................. | L. | Nov. | 3, 1844 |
| 296 | " | | Avery, George .................... | W. | Dec. | 14, 1849 |
| 296 | " | | Avery, Aliada R................... | G. | Aug. | 20, 1873 |
| 298 | " | | Wheeler, George................... | * | Oct. | 1, 1847 |
| 299 | " | | Dempsey, Francis .. ............... | G. | Feb. | 20, 1872 |
| 300 | April 30, 1843. | L. | Earl, Mary ....................... | L. | March | 17, 1845 |
| 301 | " | | McMaster, Isabella................. | | .......... | |
| 302 | " | C | Stafford, John D ................. | W. | July | 1845 |
| 303 | " | | Stafford, Rachel.................. | L. | March | 20, 1846 |
| 304 | " | | McMaster, William.... ........... | W. | April | 17, 1846 |
| 305 | " | | Harwood, Harvey.................. | W. | May | 24, 1850 |
| 306 | " | | Miller, Lucy. . .................. | W. | May | 2, 1847 |
| 307 | " | | Harford, Maria.................... | L. | May | 22, 1843 |
| 308 | June 25, 1843. | C. | Sherman, David A.................. | W. | April | 23, 1852 |
| 309 | " | | Fursman, William Henry........... | W. | May | 24, 1850 |
| 310 | " | L | Woolcott, Louisa G ............... | * | June | 28, 1850 |
| 311 | " | | Johnson, Lucy .................... | L. | Oct. | 11, 1845 |
| 312 | Aug. 27, 1843. | L. | Pratt, Calvin..................... | L. | May | 2, 1844 |
| 313 | " | | Pratt, Lemantha .................. | | " | |
| 314 | " | | Pratt, Juliette.................... | | " | |
| 315 | " | C. | Childs, Julia A. ................. | L. | March | 12, 2854 |
| 316 | Oct. 29, 1843. | L. | McComb, Margaret (Wright).......... | L | Aug. | 8, 1849 |
| 317 | " | C. | Sherman, Harriet ................. | L. | .......... | |
| 318 | Dec. 31, 1843. | L | Case, Viola....................... | L. | Sept. | 24, 1855 |
| 319 | " | | Newhall, Melissa M ............... | L. | Nov. | 3, 1844 |
| 320 | Dec. 29, 1844. | C. | Keep, Dwight .................... | * | April | 16, 1869 |
| 321 | June 29, 1845. | L. | Nicholls, Hezekiah W ............. | | .......... | |

## MEMBERS OF THE CHURCH (*Continued*).

| NO. | RECEIVED. | | SUBSEQUENT ADDITIONS. | | REMOVAL. | |
|---|---|---|---|---|---|---|
| 322 | June 29. 1845. | L | Nicholls, Pamelia...................... | | ................. | |
| 323 | " | | Place, Charlotte, Mrs... ............ | * | Aug. | 7, 1883 |
| 324 | " | | Russell, Isaac H...................... | L. | April | 17, 1846 |
| 325 | " | | Russel, Ann.......................... | | " | |
| 326 | Sept. 7, 1845. | L. | Hatch, Lucy.......................... | L. | Feb. | 26, 1847 |
| 327 | " | | Hatch, Helen N. (Streeter)......... | L. | Sept. | 19, 1847 |
| 328 | " | | Hatch, Augusta....................... | L. | Feb. | 26, 1857 |
| 329 | " | C. | Maxwell, Sarah C ............. .......... | L. | Oct. | 11, 1845 |
| 330 | Oct 26, 1845. | L. | Barrett, Sophia ..................... | L. | June | 16, 1856 |
| 331 | Dec, 28, 1845. | L. | Cantine, Mary M. (Woodworth)........ | * | June | 20, 1855 |
| 332 | Mar. 1, 1846. | L. | Harmony, Cornelia C................. | * | Aug. | 14, 1873 |
| 333 | " | | Harroun, Emily C.................... | G. | Feb. | 20, 1872 |
| 334 | " | | Kingsley, Cornelia C. (Fisher)........ | * | Feb. | 20, 1872 |
| 345 | Apr. 19, 1846. | L. | Webber, Chloe....................... | L. | Aug. | 29, 1849 |
| 336 | " | | Webber, Almena...................... | | " | |
| 337 | " | | Carpenter, Lucy...................... | | " | |
| 338 | " | | Newhall, Elbridge G................. | * | Sept. | 1852 |
| 339 | June 28, 1846. | L. | Whiting, Abby.. ................... | L. | June | 22. 1849 |
| 340 | " | | Bennett, Francis E................. | L. | Oct. | 27, 1857 |
| 341 | " | | Keep, Flavia W...................... | * | April | 11, 1882 |
| 342 | Apr. 25, 1847. | L. | Chapman, Garden S.................. | L. | June | 16, 1858 |
| 343 | " | | Chapman, Amanda.................... | | " | |
| 344 | " | | Perkins, Eliza B ................... | L. | Aug. | 18, 1851 |
| 345 | " | C. | Durfee, Samuel G.................. | L. | Jan. | 9, 1865 |
| 346 | " | | Fursman, Almira (King) .............. | L. | March | 30, 1849 |
| 347 | Sept. 29, 1847. | L. | Davis, Edward W ................. | L. | Dec. | 27. 1850 |
| 348 | Oct. 31, 1847. | L. | Goodrich, Eliza Ann................. | * | April | 21, 1871 |
| 349 | " | | Cady, Catharine...................... | | .................. | |
| 350 | " | | Clark, Charlotte C. (Fox)............. | L. | Dec. | 14, 1841 |
| 351 | Apr. 23, 1848. | L. | Clark, Alpheus...................... | * | Nov. | 16, 1874 |
| 352 | " | | Clark, Anna......................... | | ................. | |
| 353 | " | | White, Jennette S.................. | L. | July | 18, 1849 |
| 354 | " | | Evans, Lucinda ................... | * | | 1857 |
| 355 | Apr. 30, 1848. | L. | White, Mary ...................... | | ................. | |
| 356 | " | | Moore, Charlotte A ................ | | ................. | |
| 357 | Oct. 29, 1848. | L. | Gaylord, Luman R.................. | L. | June | 24. 1853 |
| 358 | " | | Gaylord, Catharine M................. | | " | |
| 359 | " | | Crocker, Sarah M................... | | ................. | |
| 360 | " | | Clapp, Mary M...................... | L. | Dec. | 1865 |
| 361 | " | C. | Clapp, James R .................... | | " | |
| 362 | Dec. 29, 1848. | L. | Pomroy, John...................... | * | July | 30, 1851 |
| 363 | " | | Pomroy, Deborah .................. | * | June | 9, 1851 |
| 364 | Sept. 27, 1849. | L. | Kingsbury, Horace.... | L. | Oct. | 13, 1853 |
| 365 | Dec. 28, 1849. | L. | Prudden, Henry..................... | L. | Aug. | 25. 1854 |
| 366 | " | | Prudden, Sarah A................... | | " | |
| 367 | " | | Webber, Thomas W ................ | * | Dec. | 5, 1874 |
| 368 | " | | Webber, Laura M .................. | * | Jan. | 12, 1879 |
| 369 | " | | Gilman, Edward W.................. | L. | June | 11, 1856 |
| 370 | " | | Judd, Rhoda (Raymond) ............. | | ................. | |
| 371 | " | | Raymond, Augustus E............ | * | Sept. | 3, 1874 |
| 372 | " | | Powell, Thomas B .................. | L. | Nov. | 9, 1851 |
| 373 | " | C. | Flagler, Phebe L. (Wentworth)........ | | .................. | |
| 374 | " | | Goodrich, Frances E (Clark)....... | | | |
| 375 | " | | Stewart, Sarah C.................... | L. | April | 14, 1860 |
| 376 | Feb. 22, 1850. | C. | Tracy, Marilla..................... | * | Dec. | 27, 1872 |
| 377 | " | L. | Tyler, Maria .... ................... | L. | Jan. | 29, 1872 |
| 378 | Apr. 26, 1850. | L. | Gould, William B ................. | | .................. | |

---

## MEMBERS OF THE CHURCH (*Continued*).

| NO. | RECEIVED. | | SUBSEQUENT ADDITIONS. | | REMOVAL. | |
|---|---|---|---|---|---|---|
| 379 | April 26, 1850. | L. | Connitt, George W. | L. | Nov. | 19, 1857 |
| 380 | " | | Knight, Betsey D. | * | Nov. | 11, 1878 |
| 381 | " | C. | Griffin, Margaret. | L. | Jan. | 4, 1854 |
| 382 | July 5, 1850. | L. | Goodrich, Isaac G. | L. | Oct. | 25, 1850 |
| 383 | " | | Townsend, George B | | | |
| 384 | " | | Townsend, Lucinda. | | | |
| 385 | " | C. | Cole, Cornelius | L. | Oct. | 1, 1854 |
| 386 | " | | Moody, Elisha. | | | |
| 387 | " | | Moody, Margaret. | * | Nov. | 29, 1881 |
| 388 | " | | Goodrich, Loretta. | L. | April | 27, 1851 |
| 389 | " | | Bloomfield, Mary Eliza. | * | Dec. | 27, 1864 |
| 390 | Aug. 23, 1850. | L. | Leonard, Rufus. | * | Feb. | 5, 1853 |
| 391 | " | | Leonard, Esther. | L. | Aug. | 26, 1853 |
| 392 | " | | Cole, Phileta C. | L. | Oct. | 1, 1854 |
| 393 | " | | Carney, Mary J. | L. | July | 16, 1856 |
| 394 | " | | Holt, Almira S. | * | June | 25, 1871 |
| 395 | Oct. 27, 1850. | C. | Parker, Maria B. | * | May | 7, 1853 |
| 396 | " | | Brown, Betsey R. | L. | May | 3, 1865 |
| 397 | " | | Gilman, Julia S. | L. | June | 11, 1856 |
| 398 | Dec. 27, 1850. | L. | Bacon, Austin S. | L. | Nov. | 7, 1852 |
| 399 | " | | Bacon, Lana. | " | | |
| 400 | Feb. 23, 1851. | C. | Whitcher, Ellen O. (Richardson) | | | |
| 401 | Apr. 25, 1851. | L. | Brown, Levi. | L. | Dec. | 15, 1854 |
| 402 | " | | Brown, Eliza. | " | | |
| 403 | Aug. 29, 1851. | L. | Stewart, Harriet (Judd). | L. | June | 6, 1855 |
| 404 | Apr. 25, 1852. | C. | Newhall, Lucy E. (Hall). | L. | June | 24, 1853 |
| 405 | " | | Levan, Eliza A. (Campbell) | L | | |
| 406 | " | | Moore, Benjamin C | * | March | 21, 1877 |
| 407 | " | | Moore, Sarah Ann | | | |
| 408 | " | | Brown, Sylinda M. | L | Dec. | 15, 1854 |
| 409 | " | | Gould, Julia A. | | | |
| 410 | " | C. | Ferguson, James. | G. | Feb. | 20, 1872 |
| 411 | " | | Ferguson, Ann. | L. | Dec. | 31, 1862 |
| 412 | June 27, 1852. | C. | Leonard, Alice M. | * | Oct. | 9, 1854 |
| 413 | " | L. | Murray, Daniel R | L. | Oct. | 5, 1850 |
| 414 | " | | Murray, Algina B | | | " |
| 415 | " | | Crocker, Charles A | L. | April | 9, 1856 |
| 416 | " | C. | Stedman, Frances (Gould). | G | May | 11, 1877 |
| 417 | Aug. 27, 1852. | L. | Allen, Elizabeth Ann (McCollum) | W. | April | 28, 1854 |
| 418 | Oct. 31, 1852. | C. | Holmes, Frances A. (Marsh). | L. | March | 1861 |
| 419 | " | | Place, Mary C. (Nesmith). | G. | Feb. | 20, 1872 |
| 420 | Dec. 26, 1852. | C. | Moore, Lucia O. | L. | April | 28, 1854 |
| 421 | Feb. 25, 1853. | L. | Leonard, Delevan L. | L. | Aug. | 13, 1871 |
| 422 | Apr. 24, 1853. | C. | Duncan, Frances (Doolittle) | L | | 1866 |
| 423 | " | | Newhall, Sarah L. (Babcock) | | | |
| 424 | Apr. 23, 1853. | L. | Whitmore, Anna F., Mrs. | * | Feb. | 20, 1873 |
| 425 | Apr. 22, 1853. | L. | Wright, Margaret, Mrs | | | |
| 426 | " | | Simmons, Walter | | | |
| 427 | " | | Van Tassel, Lucy E | L. | Jan. | 3, 1865 |
| 428 | June 26, 1853. | C. | Harwood, Julia A. (Strong). | L. | | 1863 |
| 429 | June 24, 1853. | L. | Hubbard, Mary A | L. | April | 18, 1885 |
| 430 | Aug 26, 1853. | L. | Judd, Mary | L. | | |
| 431 | " | | Judd, Laura (Post) | L. | | |
| 432 | Dec. 25, 1853. | C. | Curtis, Esther A. (Nicholls). | L. | May | 20, 1857 |
| 433 | Apr. 30, 1854. | C. | Howell, Mary J | G. | Aug | 20, 1873 |
| 434 | " | | Chapman, Pruella R | L. | June | 16, 1858 |
| 435 | Apr. 28, 1854. | L | Dill, Elizabeth | * | June | 22, 1861 |

## MEMBERS OF THE CHURCH (Continued).

| NO. | RECEIVED. | SUBSEQUENT MEMBERS. | | REMOVED. | |
|---|---|---|---|---|---|
| 436 | Nov. 19, 1854. | L. Morse, James H. | L. | Jan. | 30, 1856 |
| 437 | " | Morse, Harriet S. | | " | |
| 438 | " | Morse, Edward | | " | |
| 439 | " | Morse, Abigail | | " | |
| 440 | Jan. 21, 1855. | L. Kingsbury, Horace | | | |
| 441 | April 27, 1855. | L. Robbins, Harriet M. | L. | Feb. | .., 1856 |
| 442 | April 29, 1855. | C. Northam, Laura A. | * | Dec. | 3, 1859 |
| 443 | July 1, 1855. | C. Papworth, George | G. | Aug. | 20, 1873 |
| 444 | " | Doty, Mary J. | L. | Aug. | 23, 1857 |
| 445 | June 30, 1855. | L. Jones, John T. | L. | July | 2, 1855 |
| 446 | " | Parker, Elijah | * | Feb. | 8, 1868 |
| 447 | " | Prudden, Henry | L | June | 29, 1870 |
| 448 | " | Prudden, Sarah | | " | |
| 449 | Aug. 24, 1855. | L. Brown, Samuel B | L. | June | 25, 1862 |
| 450 | " | Brown, Sophronia S. | | " | |
| 451 | " | Prudden, George N. | G. | Aug. | 20, 1873 |
| 452 | " | Prudden, Mary F. | | " | |
| 453 | Dec. 28, 1855. | L. Wilkinson, America | L. | June | 23, 1856 |
| 454 | Feb. 22, 1856. | L. Gates, Joseph J. | L. | Dec. | .., 1865 |
| 455 | " | Gates, Isabella R. | | " | |
| 456 | " | Hollister, Mervin | * | | |
| 457 | June 29, 1856. | C. Northam, Cyrus C | L. | Jan. | 2, 1870 |
| 458 | Aug. 29, 1856. | L. Day, Marian W., Mrs. | L. | Oct. | 29, 1884 |
| 459 | Nov. 14, 1856. | L. Judson, Silas | L. | Nov. | 25, 1857 |
| 460 | Oct. 25, 1857. | L. Robbins, Caroline | L. | June | 22, 1873 |
| 461 | " | Bennett, Joseph L. | L. | Jan. | 18, 1871 |
| 462 | " | Bennett, Eliza A | L. | April | 26, 1871 |
| 463 | Dec. 25, 1857. | L. Goodrich, Martha S. | L. | March | 3, 1865 |
| 464 | Feb. 25, 1858. | L. Macomber, Mrs. | | " | |
| 465 | Feb. 28, 1859. | C. Macomber, Miss. | | " | |
| 466 | April 25, 1858. | C. Blackley, Richard | | | |
| 467 | " | Blackley, Susan, Mrs. | | | |
| 468 | " | Barr, Gabriel | * | April | 12, 1866 |
| 469 | " | Brazee, Mary E | L. | March | 2, 1877 |
| 470 | " | Crocker, Daniel P. | | | |
| 471 | " | Crocker, Orpha E. | | | |
| 472 | " | Rennett, Elizabeth (Wheaton) | | | |
| 473 | " | Moore, Sarah E. | G. | May | 11, 1877 |
| 474 | " | Brown, Aurelia L. | L | Feb. | 20, 1879 |
| 475 | " | Holmes, Kate A. (Haines) | | | |
| 476 | " | Parker, Charles F. | G. | May | 11, 1877 |
| 477 | " | Hibbard, Lovedy, Mrs. A. J. | | | |
| 478 | " | Dunton, Austin | L. | Sept. | 17, 1882 |
| 479 | " | Brown, Eliza | L. | Feb. | 14, 1872 |
| 480 | " | Crocker, J. Newton | L. | Jan. | 1, 1869 |
| 481 | " | Crocker, Hannah S. | | | |
| 482 | " | Nicholls, Mary F. (Olds | | | |
| 483 | " | Moore, Anna P. (Trevor) | | | |
| 484 | " | Holmes, Helen E. (Charlton) | L | Oct. | 24, 1862 |
| 485 | " | Parker, Albert B. | G. | May | 11, 1877 |
| 486 | " | Moody, Ellen R. (Scott) | | | |
| 487 | " | Fitch, Hannah | | | |
| 488 | " | Biter, Barbary (Long) | | | |
| 489 | " | Townsend, Sophia | | | |
| 490 | " | Belden, Angeline G. | | | |
| 491 | " | Hammer, Kate B. | G. | May | 6, 1874 |
| 492 | " | Rood, Porter J. | * | Nov. | 19, 1875 |

## MEMBERS OF THE CHURCH (*Continued*).

| NO. | RECEIVED. | SUBSEQUENT MEMBERS. | REMOVED. | | |
|---|---|---|---|---|---|
| 493 | April 25, 1858. | C. Rood, Abbie............................................ | | | |
| 494 | " | Dunn, Frances E. (Griseen)............ | L. | June | 30, 1880 |
| 495 | " | Gooding, Ada F............ ............. | L. | May | 12, 1869 |
| 496 | " | Graham, Almon M.......................... | | | |
| 497 | " | Graham, Mary............................... | L. | April | 23, 1884 |
| 498 | " | Hibbard, A. Judson....................... | | | |
| 499 | " | Green, Emma F............................. | W. | Jan. | 8, 1873 |
| 500 | " | Knight, George P........................... | | | |
| 501 | " | Knight, Phila A.............................. | | | |
| 502 | " | Moody, George H............................ | | | |
| 503 | " | Clark, Alpheus B............................ | W. | Aug. | 13, 1884 |
| 504 | " | Fitzgerald, David........................... | * | July | 9, 1858 |
| 505 | " | Tracy, Elisha................................. | L. | June | 10, 1885 |
| 506 | " | Tracy, Maria L. (Thompson)............ | L | May | 12, 1869 |
| 507 | " | Lester, Eliza................................. | L. | Jan. | 11, 1865 |
| 508 | " | Wicks, Martha M........................... | G. | Feb. | 20, 1872 |
| 509 | " | Daniels, Lucy (Depew)..................... | | | |
| 510 | " | Simmons, Helen L.......................... | * | Feb. | ... 1863 |
| 511 | " | Dill, Deborah (Woodyear)............... | * | Aug. | 11, 1880 |
| 512 | " | Raymond, Philena ........... ........... | | July | 17, 1866 |
| 513 | " | Collier, Mary E.............................. | L. | July | 5, 1876 |
| 514 | " | Blinn, Frances E. (Smith)............... | L. | Nov. | 27, 1878 |
| 515 | " | Rood, Charles S............................. | L. | April | 8, 1885 |
| 516 | " | Rood, Phebe A. (Curtis)................. | L. | April | 20, 1871 |
| 517 | " | Moore, Libbie H............................. | | | |
| 518 | " | L. Jacobs, Emma............................... | L. | April | 26, 1871 |
| 519 | " | Dunton, Helen M.. ...... .......... | L. | Sept. | 17, 1882 |
| 520 | " | Wilkineon, Sarah (Davidson).......... | * | Nov. | ... 1865 |
| 521 | June 27, 1858. | C. Smith, Andrew............................... | L. | July | 21, 1880 |
| 522 | " | Burrell, Arthur............................. | L. | Aug. | 20, 1879 |
| 523 | " | Nicholls, George ........................ | L. | Aug. | 22, 1875 |
| 524 | " | Gates, Eliza W............................... | .. | Oct. | 26, 1860 |
| 525 | " | Dill, Catharine B. (Hildreth)........... | L. | Jan. | 17, 1883 |
| 526 | " | Hess, Mary, Mrs............................ | * | Mch. | 21, 1882 |
| 527 | June 16, 1858. | L. Ayer, Delilah................................ | L. | Feb. | 28, 1868 |
| 528 | " | Ayer, Eliza................................... | L. | Oct. | 19, 1859 |
| 529 | " | Ayer, Henry H............................... | L. | Jan. | 3, 1872 |
| 530 | Aug. 27, 1858. | C. Gilrie, Alexander. .............. ........... | * | Jan. | 31, 1873 |
| 531 | " | Gilrie, Sarah ................................ | * | Aug. | 9, 1865 |
| 532 | Oct. ..., 1858. | L. Daly, Mrs................................... | G. | Feb. | 20, 1872 |
| 533 | " | Wilkinson, James A......................... | G. | Aug. | 20, 1873 |
| 534 | " | Wilkinson, Mary W......................... | | | " |
| 535 | June 24, 1859. | L. Stevens, Alexander H..................... | L. | Nov. | 30, 1859 |
| 536 | " | Stevens, Mrs. A. H.... . ......... | | | " |
| 537 | " | Stevens, Julia............................... | | | " |
| 538 | Oct. 29, 1859. | L. Morgan, Lavinia ...................... | * | Feb. | 1, 1871 |
| 539 | Dec. 25, 1859. | C. Campbell, Mary.......................... | * | July | 7, 1884 |
| 540 | Feb. 24, 1860. | L. Holbrook, Amos.......................... | | | |
| 541 | " | Holbrook, Ellen S. ................... | | | |
| 542 | April 27, 1860. | C. Smith, Adeline L. D. (Jackson)........ | L. | Dec. | 24, 1871 |
| 543 | April 29, 1860. | C. Pasco, Mary.............................. | * | Oct. | 4, 1871 |
| 544 | " | Pasco, Edward.............................. | * | Mch. | 17, 1876 |
| 545 | " | Marsh, Lydia M............................. | L. | Aug. | 30, 1876 |
| 546 | " | Marsh, Burton .............................. | L. | Feb. | 11, 1877 |
| 547 | " | Lane, Asher.................................. | G. | May | 11, 1877 |
| 548 | " | Lamb, Louisa C............................. | | | " |
| 549 | " | Penfield, Ambrose B.... ........... ..... | L. | June | 29, 1862 |

## MEMBERS OF THE CHURCH (*Continued*).

| NO. | RECEIVED. | SUBSEQUENT MEMBERS. | | REMOVED. |
|---|---|---|---|---|
| 550 | April 29, 1860. | C. Penfield, Diana | L. | June 29, 1862 |
| 551 | " | Penfield, Charles R. | | " |
| 552 | Dec. 30, 1860. | C. Adkins, Elizabeth A. | * | Feb. 3, 1876 |
| 553 | Aug. 23, 1861. | L. Brown, Dennison D. | L | Dec. 20, 1876 |
| 554 | " | Brown, Sarah | | " |
| 555 | Oct 27, 1861. | C. Brown, Harriet | L. | Dec. 24, 1863 |
| 556 | June 27, 1862. | L. Numan, Harriet, Miss | L. | Sept. .., 1883 |
| 557 | " | Rewey, George | L. | |
| 558 | June 29, 1862. | C. Saraw, Bartholomew | W. | July 16, 1884 |
| 559 | " | Saraw, Margaret | | |
| 560 | Oct. 24, 1862. | L. Lerch, Nathaniel | | |
| 561 | Dec. 26, 1862. | L. Lord, Eliza A., Mrs. | * | Dec. 25, 1863 |
| 562 | " | Clift, John W. | | |
| 563 | " | Clift, Lucy C. | | |
| 564 | Dec. 28, 1862. | C. Clark, Harriet S. (Robbins) | L. | Feb. 11, 1877 |
| 565 | Feb. 20, 1863. | L. Ransom, Newell K. | L. | Dec. 1, 1867 |
| 566 | " | Ransom, Mary B. | | " |
| 567 | April 24, 1863. | L. Dingman, Catharine | * | April 23, 1878 |
| 568 | June 26, 1863. | L. Cass, Aaron | * | ..... ..., 1865 |
| 569 | " | Cass, Hannah | L. | Feb. 4, 1872 |
| 570 | " | Harrington, Lucy | * | Dec. 24, 1873 |
| 571 | " | Gould, Aaron M. | L. | June .., 1865 |
| 572 | " | Gould, Mary A. | | " |
| 573 | June 28, 1863. | C. Carrier, Lucy, Mrs. | | |
| 574 | Dec. 27, 1863. | C. Lerch, Frances | | |
| 575 | Feb. 26, 1864. | L. Penfield, Ambrose B. | | |
| 576 | " | Penfield, Diana. | * | April 21, 1877 |
| 577 | " | Penfield, Chas. R. | | |
| 578 | " | Hilton. Elizabeth E. | | |
| 579 | April 20, 1864. | L. Ayer, Eliza | L. | Nov. 26, 1871 |
| 580 | " | Harrington, Louisa (Seeley) | L. | Aug. 6, 1871 |
| 581 | July 1, 1864. | L. Wilson, Helena M. | L. | July 24, 1872 |
| 582 | " | Evans, Agnes W. | | |
| 583 | " | Freeman, Clarissa | * | Dec. 17, 1867 |
| 584 | Jan. 1, 1865. | C. Minard, Amanda | L. | Jan. 5, 1870 |
| 585 | May 5, 1865. | L. Hough, Dennis | L. | Sept, 17, 1884 |
| 586 | " | Hough, Alletta | | " |
| 587 | June 30, 1865. | L. Harris, Charlotte M. | * | Feb. 3, 1871 |
| 588 | Sept. 1, 1865. | L. Cushing, Sarah L., Mrs. | | |
| 589 | Sept. 3, 1865. | C. Leonard, Sarah J. | L. | April 26, 1871 |
| 590 | Mch. 2, 1866. | L. Williard, Abigail | G. | Feb. 20, 1872 |
| 591 | " | Cook, Hiram A. | * | Feb. 24, 1884 |
| 592 | " | Cook, Lucinda | | |
| 593 | May 13, 1866. | C. Stace, Jenney H. | G. | July 2, 1875 |
| 594 | " | Holt, Emma J. | L. | March 24, 1883 |
| 595 | " | Parker, Mary J. | * | Aug. 24, 1866 |
| 596 | " | Balliet, William D. | | |
| 597 | " | Tyler, George | L. | Jan. 14, 1871 |
| 598 | " | Adkins, Joseph L. | | |
| 599 | " | Perrigo, George W. | L. | April 1, 1877 |
| 600 | " | Raymond, Charles A. | L. | March 2, 1877 |
| 601 | " | Rood. Curtis. | | |
| 602 | " | Graham, William J. | | |
| 603 | " | Trevor. William W. | | |
| 604 | " | Marsh, Charles A. | L. | Dec. 13, 1868 |
| 605 | " | Windsor, William | | |
| 606 | " | Richardson, Eliza C. (Chapin) | | |

## MEMBERS OF THE CHURCH (*Continued*).

| NO. | RECEIVED. | SUBSEQUENT MEMBERS. | | REMOVED. |
|---|---|---|---|---|
| 607 | May 13, 1866. | C. Finn, Jane T............................ | * | Sept. 26, 1879 |
| 608 | " | Dunning, Elizabeth .... ............. | | ............ |
| 609 | " | Carpenter, Melinda. ... .......... | L. | Feb. 19, 1873. |
| 610 | " | Moore, Emma (Penfield)............. | | ............ |
| 611 | " | Windsor, Isabella......... | | ............ |
| 612 | " | Blair, Mary (Morrell)......... | | ... |
| 613 | " | Birdsall, Harriet. ............ | | |
| 614 | " | Crocker, Alice E. ......... | | |
| 615 | " | Holmes, Anna C. (Colby)............. | L. | Dec. 11. 1878 |
| 616 | " | Stone, Almira........................ | * | May 24, 1870 |
| 617 | " | Bowman, Ernestine................ .. | * | Dec. 30, 1870 |
| 618 | " | White, Angeline ..... | | ............ |
| 619 | " | Perry, Anna Lord, Mrs. ........... | | |
| 620 | " | Tyler, Elizabeth S.......... .. | L. | Aug. 17, 1873 |
| 621 | " | Holbrook, Ella M (Moody)........... | | |
| 622 | " | Cady, Anna E. (Mackey) ............. | | |
| 623 | " | Burrell, Ellen.... ............. | L. | June 11, 1871 |
| 624 | " | Colt, Sarah E........................ | G. | May 11, 1877 |
| 625 | " | Gooding, Harriet (Fitts)....... . | | |
| 626 | " | Whitcher, Harriet (Ballou)........... | L. | Jan. 7, 1885 |
| 627 | " | Wright, Alice B. ......... | | ............ |
| 628 | " | Haines, Calvin ..... | | ............ |
| 629 | " | Stockwell, James K................... | G. | May 11, 1877 |
| 630 | " | Nelson. Calvin... .............. | L. | May 4, 1877 |
| 631 | " | Blair, William........... | * | Sept. 26, 1874 |
| 632 | " | Graham, Emma, Mrs. Wm. J.......... | | ............ |
| 633 | " | Rowell. Charles W......... .. | G. | May 2, 1884 |
| 634 | " | Pickard. Elizabeth C. ......... | | ............ |
| 635 | " | Brink, Melissa J..................... | | |
| 636 | " | Lane, Alfaretta.... ............. | L. | ..... .., 1867 |
| 637 | " | Hibbard, Melissa (Trude).... ....... | L. | Nov. 19, 1879 |
| 638 | " | Campbell, Deborah (Smith)......... | L. | Oct. 25, 1874 |
| 639 | " | Higgins, Joseph W.... ... ...... | | ............ |
| 640 | " | Stukins, Charles....... | | ............ |
| 641 | " | O'Keefe, William H............... | | ............ |
| 642 | " | Allen, A. Judson.................. | | ............ |
| 643 | " | Walter, Delilah ..................... | L. | Jan. 18, 1871 |
| 644 | " | Rowell, Emma (Atwood)............ | | |
| 645 | " | Crapsey, Jane (Barnes)............ | | |
| 646 | " | Crapsey, Addie (Rood) ... ......... | L. | April 8, 1885 |
| 647 | " | Simmons. Esther L. ............ . | | |
| 648 | " | Lane, Abby ..... ............ | L. | June .., 1867 |
| 649 | " | Oliver, Isa B. (Baker)............. | L. | June 23, 1880 |
| 650 | " | Sheldon. Harriet (Browning)....... | L. | April 7, 1875 |
| 651 | " | Dingman, Delilah (Makepeace)........ | L. | March 2, 1877 |
| 652 | " | Leet, Harriet (Sullivan) ..... ....... | L. | Feb. 27, 1874 |
| 653 | " | Gooding, Nellie B........ | | |
| 654 | " | Perrigo, Emma, Mrs.. ......... | L. | April 1, 1877 |
| 655 | " | Richardson, Salome E. (Moyer)........ | | |
| 656 | " | L. Thompson, George F. ............ | G. | May 6, 1874 |
| 657 | " | Thompson, Cornelia B............. | | " |
| 658 | " | Weaver, Erastus B............... | | |
| 659 | " | Weaver, Louisa E , Mrs........... | | ... ............ |
| 660 | " | Letch, Jeremiah E................ | | ............ |
| 661 | " | Brink, Della, Mrs.. ............... | | |
| 662 | " | Blair, Mary, Mrs................ | * | Nov. 23, 1879 |
| 663 | " | Hyde, Mary..................... | G. | May 11, 1877 |

90

## MEMBERS OF THE CHURCH (*Continued*).

| NO. | RECEIVED. | | SUBSEQUENT MEMBERS. | | REMOVED. |
|---|---|---|---|---|---|
| 664 | May 13, 1866. | L. | Huntley, Willis J. | L. | Sept 24, 1879 |
| 665 | " | | Trowbridge. Emily, Mrs. W. | | |
| 666 | " | | Macartney, S. J., Mrs. | L. | Nov. 1, 1867 |
| 667 | " | | White, Emily M. | * | May 14, 1882 |
| 668 | " | | Rowell, Eliza, Mrs. | * | March 5, 1875 |
| 669 | July 1, 1866. | C. | Moody, Calista L. | | |
| 670 | " | | Carpenter, Harriet | L. | May 12, 1869 |
| 671 | " | | Ferguson, Mary. | * | Nov. 2, 1875 |
| 672 | " | | Ferguson, Almeda (Brown). | | |
| 673 | " | | Farwell, Ella (Duncan) | | |
| 674 | " | | Austin, Edward D. | L. | Dec. 12, 1873 |
| 675 | " | | Ayer, Erastus. | L. | May 8, 1870 |
| 676 | " | | Craw. Alason. | L. | May 24, 1871 |
| 677 | " | | Stukins. Elizabeth, Mrs. | | |
| 678 | " | | Finn, Elizabeth (Scarborough). | L. | Feb. 22, 1874 |
| 679 | " | | Tyler, Marcus. | L. | Aug. 17, 1873 |
| 680 | " | | Gooding, Augustus Stewart | | |
| 681 | " | | Ferguson, Sarah. | L. | Dec. 26, 1869 |
| 682 | Nov. 2, 1866. | L. | Briggs, Mary L. | L. | June 10, 1868 |
| 683 | " | | Glover, William | L. | April 17, 1872 |
| 684 | " | | Glover, Elizabeth. | | " |
| 685 | " | | Glover, Anna. | * | Jan. 29. 1879 |
| 686 | " | | Glover, Margaretta (Lovell). | | |
| 687 | Jan. 4, 1867. | L. | Allen, Nathaniel H. | | |
| 688 | " | | Allen, Nancy M. | | |
| 689 | May 3, 1867. | L. | Pierce, Sarah J. | L. | April 23, 1876 |
| 690 | May 5, 1867. | C. | Raymond, Wilbur S. | L. | March 2. 1877 |
| 691 | " | | Raymond, George P. | | |
| 692 | July 7, 1867. | C. | Holmes, Lizzie S. | | |
| 693 | July 5, 1867. | L. | Thornton, Henry. | | |
| 694 | " | | Thornton. Emeline B. | * | Nov. 1, 1874 |
| 695 | Jan. 3, 1868. | L. | Holmes. Elizabeth. | | |
| 696 | " | | Baker, Palmer N. | L. | April 1, 1868 |
| 697 | " | | Baker. Lucinda. | | " |
| 698 | " | | Baker, Alice M. | | " |
| 699 | May 3, 1868. | C. | Mackey, Eliza J., Mrs. | | |
| 700 | " | | Gaskill, Olive. Mrs. | L. | July 16, 1884 |
| 701 | " | | Phelps, Lucinda (Ingham). | L. | Jan. 22, 1873 |
| 702 | " | | Phelps, Amanda M. (Silsby). | L | Sept. 8, 1880 |
| 703 | " | | Fitts, James F. | | |
| 704 | " | | Batten. Charles D. | G. | May 11, 1877 |
| 705 | " | | Mahanna, Edward. | G | |
| 706 | " | | Crocker, Robert. | | |
| 707 | " | | Carpenter, John. | L. | Feb. 19, 1873 |
| 708 | July 5, 1868. | C. | Graber, Julia (King). | | |
| 709 | " | | Stahl, Elizabeth. | | |
| 710 | Sept. 6, 1868. | L. | Gilchrist, John. | L. | July 19, 1871 |
| 711 | " | | Gilchrist, Emily. | | " |
| 712 | Mch. 19, 1869. | L. | Bennett, Edwin M. | G. | May 11, 1877 |
| 713 | " | | Bennett, Julia A. | * | Feb. 16, 1872 |
| 714 | " | | Baldwin, Electa H., Mrs. | | |
| 715 | " | | Baldwin. Rachel | * | April 14, 1883 |
| 716 | " | | Payne. Cornelia B., Mrs. | * | March 18, 1879 |
| 717 | " | | Scott, Emily M. | L. | Feb. 28, 1875 |
| 718 | " | | Graves, Edmund F. | L. | Aug. .., 1871 |
| 719 | " | | Crapsey, George. | W. | Nov. 21, 1876 |
| 720 | " | | Crapsey, Martha S. | L. | Oct. 24, 1877 |

## MEMBERS OF THE CHURCH (*Continued*).

| NO. | RECEIVED. | SUBSEQUENT MEMBERS. | | REMOVED. |
|---|---|---|---|---|
| 721 | Mch. 21, 1869. | C. Hartwell, John B. | L. | March 27, 1878 |
| 722 | " | Hartwell, Lydia P. | | " |
| 723 | " | Hibbard, Ella (Talbot). | L. | April 5, 1885 |
| 724 | " | Mapes, Harriet E., Mrs Wm. | L. | Nov. 5, 1879 |
| 725 | " | Mapes, Elizabeth F. (Houston) | L. | July 31, 1879 |
| 726 | " | Winagle, Olive, Mrs. | | |
| 727 | " | Cooley, Elizabeth | | |
| 728 | " | Cooley, Emma (Turbatt) | | |
| 729 | " | Patterson, Julia | L. | May 1, 1878 |
| 730 | " | Payne, William | W. | Jan. 4, 1884 |
| 731 | " | Ives, Warren A | L. | April 4, 1877 |
| 732 | May 2, 1869. | C. Cady, Antoinette C. (Weaver) | | |
| 733 | " | Spalding, Mary | L. | May 5, 1880 |
| 734 | " | Moody, Laura | | |
| 735 | " | Wheeler, George D. | L. | Jan. 31, 1871 |
| 736 | " | Brown, Chas. C. | | |
| 737 | " | Brown, Maria R. | | |
| 738 | " | Ward, Joseph A. | | |
| 739 | " | Ward, Josephine. | | |
| 740 | " | White ey, Maggie (Ketchum) | | |
| 741 | " | Whiteley, Letitia, Mrs. | | |
| 742 | " | Ives, Frances E. | L. | April 4, 877 |
| 743 | " | Haskins, Eliza, Mrs. | | |
| 744 | " | Bryant, Louisa | * | Nov. 10, 1878 |
| 745 | " | Dingman, George W. | | |
| 746 | " | Dingman, Georgie G. (Nelson) | L. | March 11, 1877 |
| 747 | " | Moody, George A. | W. | July 4, 1884 |
| 748 | " | Babcock, Sarah E. (Balliet) | | |
| 749 | " | Willets, Adelia C., Mrs. | | |
| 750 | " | Van Wagoner, Morgan | | |
| 751 | " | Van Wagoner, Elizabeth | * | March 1, 1879 |
| 752 | " | Crampton, Hezekiah R. | * | Aug. 23, 1880 |
| 753 | " | Crampton, Almira W. | | |
| 754 | " | Currier, John L. | * | May 8, 1885 |
| 755 | " | Carrier, Frank H. | | |
| 756 | " | Seeley, Lewis W. | L. | Aug 6, 1871 |
| 757 | " | Seeley, Cyrenius H. | G. | May 2, 1884 |
| 758 | " | Lovell, Seth M. | | |
| 759 | " | Tolhurst, Thomas A. | | |
| 760 | " | Tolhurst, Elizabeth | | |
| 761 | " | Tolhurst, William. | | |
| 762 | " | Tolhurst, Thomas | * | March 27, 1871 |
| 763 | " | Tolhurst, George | | |
| 764 | " | Tolhurst, Elizabeth A. (Grant) | | |
| 765 | " | Dornen, John | * | Jan. 17, 1874 |
| 766 | " | Anderson, Thomas J | G. | May 11, 1879 |
| 767 | " | Woodyer, John. | | |
| 768 | " | Hildreth, Alphonso A. | * | Feb. 3, 1873 |
| 769 | " | Stukins, Joseph. | * | June 14, 1871 |
| 770 | " | Finn, Albert. | | |
| 771 | " | Rood, Frank | L. | April 8, 1885 |
| 772 | " | Balliet, Albert. | | |
| 773 | " | Balliet, A. Frank | | |
| 774 | " | Robertson, Gilbert | L. | March 18, 1877 |
| 775 | " | Patterson, Henry. | | |
| 776 | " | Keep, Charles D. | G. | July 14, 1875 |
| 777 | " | Mapes, William H. | L. | Nov. 6, 1879 |

## MEMBERS OF THE CHURCH (*Continued*).

| NO. | RECEIVED. | SUBSEQUENT MEMBERS. | | REMOVED. |
|---|---|---|---|---|
| 778 | May 2, 1869. | C. Moody, Edward M......................... | | |
| 779 | " | White, Joseph A....................... | G. | May 2, 1884 |
| 780 | " | Pasco, Edward E.................... | * | Feb. 15, 1880 |
| 781 | " | Tyler, Milton...................... | L. | Jan. 24, 1872 |
| 782 | " | Banner, William E.................... | G. | May 11, 1877 |
| 783 | " | Reeves, James...... ............... | | " |
| 784 | " | Johnson, Jacob H............ .......... | | " |
| 785 | " | McMaster, Ida ............... | | .................. |
| 786 | " | McMaster, Mary E. (Apling) ... ........ | * | Jan. 24, 1875 |
| 787 | " | McMaster, James M. | | .................. |
| 788 | " | Langdon, Caroline, Mrs.... | | .................. |
| 789 | " | . Langdon, Anna (Gates)...... ......... | L. | Aug. 25, 1880 |
| 790 | " | Swift, Adeline F............. ............ | L. | June 25 1873 |
| 791 | " | Bedford, Mary J. (Karshner) ........... | L. | March 19, 1879 |
| 792 | " | Keough. Mary............... | | .................. |
| 793 | " | Drake, Frances M................. | | .................. |
| 794 | " | Duquet, Mary J.... | | .................. |
| 795 | " | Duquet, Sarah J........................ | | .................. |
| 796 | " | Higgins, Sarah............... | L. | March 14, 1884 |
| 797 | " | Eshbach, Annie M.... ............ | L. | Sept. 5, 1883 |
| 798 | " | Graham, Hector J................ | | .................. |
| 799 | " | Graham, Mary J................ | * | May 1, 1873 |
| 800 | " | Bogardus, Chas. E....... . ...... | | |
| 801 | " | Weaver, George W....... .......... | | .................. |
| 802 | " | Weaver, Mary..................... | | .................. |
| 803 | " | Specht, Sarah J...................... | | .................. |
| 804 | " | Specht, Frederick W................... | * | Feb. 22. 1879 |
| 805 | " | Keizer, Lucy (Benton)................. | G. | April 31, 1880 |
| 806 | " | Price, Sarah J.......... ..... ..... | | .................. |
| 807 | " | Price, Emma E. (Carpenter)........... | | |
| 808 | " | Steele, Sarah E.................. | | |
| 809 | " | Mormon. Harriet J.................... | L. | Feb. 27, 1874 |
| 810 | " | Brink, Elvira...................... | | .................. |
| 811 | " | Dunton, Addie L. (Wilson)........... | | .................. |
| 812 | " | Mackey, Eliza J. (Dumvill )........... | | .................. |
| 813 | " | Crapsey, Florence S................. | L. | Oct. 3, 1877 |
| 814 | " | Payne, Phebe S. (Hancock)........... | | .................. |
| 815 | " | Clark. Ella (Walsworth)............. | | .................. |
| 816 | " | Bennett, Alice...................... | L. | April 26, 1871 |
| 817 | " | Allen. Emma B ................ .. | * | May 30, 1875 |
| 818 | " | Hibbard, Emma...................... | | .................. |
| 819 | " | Mapes, Alice .. ......... ........ | | .................. |
| 820 | " | Irving, Jennie..................... | * | Oct. 15, 1873 |
| 821 | " | Reed. Melissa ........ | | .................. |
| 822 | " | Trowbridge, Venelia (Weld) ........... | L. | Feb. 8, 1874 |
| 823 | " | Trowbridge, Alice R. (Wiley).......... | | .................. |
| 824 | " | Weaver, Henry E............. ... . | L. | Jan. 14, 1874 |
| 825 | " | Weaver, Maria L. Pomroy)........... | L. | March 2, 1877 |
| 826 | " | Weaver, Mary E. (Lewis)............. | L. | Oct. 27, 1872 |
| 827 | " | Jensen, Lena (Tenbrook)............. | L. | Feb. 11, 1877 |
| 828 | " | Dunning. Samuel.................... | | ............. ...... |
| 829 | " | Morrill, Ephraim K................ | | .................. |
| 830 | " | Blair, George...................... | | .................. |
| 831 | " | Hibbard, Alida A.. Mrs.......... | | .................. |
| 832 | " | Hibbard, Harvey E....... ....... | * | Feb. 7, 1873 |
| 833 | " | Gibbs, Charlotte ..................... | L. | March 27, 1778 |
| 834 | " | Richardson, Caroline...... ............ | * | May 4, 1871 |

## MEMBERS OF THE CHURCH (*Continued*).

| NO. | RECEIVED. | | SUBSEQUENT MEMBERS. | | REMOVED. | |
|---|---|---|---|---|---|---|
| 835 | May 2, 1869. | C. | Drake, George................ | * | ............... | |
| 836 | " | | Musson, Charles............... | * | Sept. | 20, 1875 |
| 837 | " | | Tuttle, Charles............... | G. | May | 11, 1877 |
| 838 | " | | Wood, Percy W................ | W. | Jan. | 4, 1884 |
| 839 | " | | Wood, Charles C.............. | G. | Sept. | 12, 1883 |
| 840 | " | | Sprague, George A............ | G. | May | 11, 1877 |
| 841 | " | | Smith, William............... | W. | April | 16, 1884 |
| 842 | " | | Parker, Edward C............. | | | |
| 843 | " | | Marshall, George A........... | G. | May | 11, 1877 |
| 844 | " | | Armstrong, Charles .......... | | | |
| 845 | " | | McCoy, George A.............. | | | |
| 846 | " | | Craig, Joseph ............... | | | |
| 847 | " | | Graham, Robert J............. | | | |
| 848 | " | | Bryant, Lucy (Hosbury) ...... | * | July | 31, 1873 |
| 849 | " | | Bowman, Mary (Kinder)........ | | | |
| 850 | " | L. | Graves, Julia................ | L. | Aug. | ..., 1871 |
| 851 | " | | Leinbaugh, Cincero R ........ | L. | Feb. | 12, 1879 |
| 852 | " | | Leinbaugh, Lovina ........... | | " | |
| 853 | " | | Phelps, Harriet A S.......... | | | |
| 854 | " | | Bayley, Almira............... | | | |
| 855 | " | | Crocker, Sarah G............. | | | |
| 856 | July 4, 1869. | C. | Babcock, Jeptha W............ | * | Oct. | 21, 1883 |
| 857 | " | | Babcock, Mary................ | * | Sept. | 28, 1869 |
| 858 | " | | Pierson, William............ | | | |
| 859 | " | | Dunkelberg, Charles.......... | L. | March 15, 2871 | |
| 860 | " | | Aal, Albert.................. | G. | March 11, 1877 | |
| 861 | " | | Newton, James A.............. | W. | Feb. | 14, 1883 |
| 862 | " | | McChesney, Emmett............ | | | |
| 863 | " | | Allen, Laurinda, Mrs......... | | | |
| 864 | " | | Johnson, Libbie.... | | | |
| 865 | " | | Johnson, Mary (Hewison)...... | L. | May | 31, 1882 |
| 866 | " | | Moss, Mary E................. | | | |
| 867 | " | | Allen, Sarah................. | L. | Nov. | 3, 1876 |
| 868 | " | | Dick, Mary................... | L. | April | 23, 1876 |
| 869 | " | | Rose, Adelaide............... | L. | June | 3, 1874 |
| 870 | " | | Rose, Josephine... | | " | |
| 871 | " | | Graham, Jennette............. | | | |
| 872 | " | | Tucker, Mary E., Mrs......... | | | |
| 873 | Nov. 5, 1869. | L. | Longworth, Mary A............ | L. | March 15, 1871 | |
| 874 | " | | Fiddler, Ruth ....... | | " | |
| 875 | " | | Fiddler, Margaret ........... | | " | |
| 876 | Nov. 7, 1869. | C. | Dick, Nicholas............... | * | Nov | 25, 1870 |
| 877 | " | | Bedford, Eliza............... | | | |
| 878 | Dec. 31, 1869. | L. | Lerch, Amelia C.............. | * | Sept. | 6, 1874 |
| 879 | March 6, 1870. | C. | Bogardus, Caroline........... | | | |
| 880 | Mch. 25, 1870. | C. | Robbins, Sampson M........... | * | April | 13, 1870 |
| 881 | May 13, 1870. | L. | Ayer, Delilah................ | L. | Jan. | 28, 1877 |
| 882 | " | C. | Wheeler, Franklin............ | L. | Jan. | 14, 1871 |
| 883 | July 1, 1870. | L. | Culver, Isaac................ | | June | 20, 1881 |
| 884 | Sept. 11, 1870. | C. | Heroy, John B................ | * | Feb. | 22, 1871 |
| 885 | " | | Heroy, Sarah J. (Sage)....... | L. | Feb. | 14, 1883 |
| 886 | " | | Heroy, Isaiah................ | | | |
| 887 | Nov. 4, 1870. | L. | Mayne, James................. | L. | May | 3, 1872 |
| 888 | " | | Mayne, Rachel................ | | " | |
| 889 | Nov. 6, 1870. | C. | Mayne, Anna.................. | | " | |
| 890 | " | | Mayne, Kettie................ | | " | |
| 891 | Dec. 30, 1880. | L. | McRae, Sarah ................ | * | Jan. | 15, 1885 |

## MEMBERS OF THE CHURCH (*Continued*).

| NO. | RECEIVED. | SUBSEQUENT MEMBERS. | | REMOVED. |
|---|---|---|---|---|
| 892 | Aug. 30, 1871. | L. Stevens, Nelson B........ ............ | L. | July 9, 1884 |
| 893 | " | Stevens, Hannah.................... | " | " |
| 894 | " | Cooper, James W........... . ...... | L. | March 17, 1878 |
| 895 | " | Cooper, Ellen H..... ............... | | " |
| 896 | " | Greaves, Jennie H.................... | L. | Oct. 27, 1872 |
| 897 | Sept. 10, 1871. | C. Weaver, Clara I................... | | |
| 898 | " | Furgason, Fannie G. (Turner)......... | L. | Dec. 19, 1879 |
| 899 | Nov. 5, 1871. | C. Raymond, Charlie B........ . ... | L. | March 2, 1977 |
| 900 | " | Gatchell, Florence J. (Prime).......... | | |
| 901 | Jan. 5, 1872. | L. Allen, Alicia H..................... | | |
| 902 | Jan. 7, 1872 | C. Knowlton, J. R........ ........... | L. | Jan. 16, 1880 |
| 903 | " | Roden, Melissa J..................... | G. | March 11, 1877 |
| 904 | " | O'Keefe, Emma..................... | | |
| 905 | " | Wood, Mary Helen (Baker)........ . | G. | May 4, 1884 |
| 906 | March 1, 1872. | L. Stewart, Thomas.... ............... | * | June 27, 1883 |
| 907 | March 3, 1872. | C. Specht, Frederick J. ... ........... | | |
| 908 | " | Gatchell, Cynthia H................... | * | Dec. 11, 1872 |
| 909 | " | Wright, Jennie E. (Barney)........... | | |
| 910 | May 3, 1872. | L. King, Sarah E..................... | * | Sept. 12, 1877 |
| 911 | May 5, 1872. | C. King, Lebbeus B................... | | |
| 912 | | Moyer Frank J............a........ | | |
| 913 | July 5, 1872. | L. Ransom, John..................... | L. | Oct. 15, 1873 |
| 914 | " | Ransom, Sylinda M................... | | " |
| 915 | " | Higgins, Sarah C. Stewart........... | | |
| 916 | " | Zimmerman, John .................... | W. | June 3, 1874 |
| 917 | " | Zimmerman, Elizabeth.............. | L. | July 26, 1876 |
| 918 | July 7, 1872. | C. Maclay, Janette H.................. | L. | Jan. 22, 1873 |
| 919 | Sept. 1, 1872. | C. Bennett, John C................... | | |
| 920 | Nov. 22, 1872. | L. Holt, Ada F...................... | | |
| 921 | Nov. 24, 1872. | C. Hartwell, John Patterson ............. | L | March 27, 1878 |
| 922 | " | Hartwell, Mary Eugenia .............. | | " |
| 923 | Jan. 3, 1873. | L. Noble, John..................... | | |
| 924 | Jan. 5, 1873. | C. Dennis, Eliza .................... | L. | Feb. 27, 1878 |
| 925 | Feb. 28, 1873. | L. Potter, Alvah K................... | | |
| 926 | " | Potter, Ellen S...................... | | |
| 927 | " | Marsh, Charles A.................... | L. | Dec. 18, 1878 |
| 928 | " | Lewis, Mary E. .................... . | L. | March 19, 1879 |
| 929 | March 2, 1873. | C. Foster, Charles.................... | L. | Sept. 13, 1876 |
| 930 | " | Day, William....................... | W. | Nov. 12, 1884 |
| 931 | " | Numan, Josie E..................... | L. | Sept. ..., 1883 |
| 932 | " | Lambert, Martha J. (Murray) ......... | | |
| 933 | " | Lambert, Sarah A. (Naismith).. ...... | | |
| 934 | May 2, 1873. | L. Chipman, Julius................... | | |
| 935 | " | Chipman, Hannah.................. | | |
| 936 | " | Chapin, Orramel S.................. | | |
| 937 | " | Mix, Maria, Mrs...... ............ | | |
| 938 | May 4, 1873. | C. Parker, Hattie Grace.. ........... | | |
| 939 | " | Gardner, Cassius M. Clay ........... | | |
| 940 | " | Gardner, Jane Laird ... ............ | | |
| 941 | " | Brown, Minnie Frances.............. | L. | Dec. 20, 1876 |
| 942 | " | Sprague, Henrietta Louisa............ | W. | Jan. 4, 1884 |
| 943 | " | Hamilton, Frances W. (Graham) ....... | | |
| 944 | " | Reed, Frances A. (Bissell)............. | L | March 28, 1883 |
| 945 | " | Windsor, Mary Libbie................ | | |
| 946 | " | Lerch, Nellie Estella................. | | |
| 947 | " | Long, Rosa M. (McGough)............ | | |
| 948 | " | Acker, Martha DeEtte................ | L. | March 7, 1877 |

## MEMBERS OF THE CHURCH (*Continued*).

| NO. | RECEIVED. | | SUBSEQUENT MEMBERS. | REMOVED. | |
|---|---|---|---|---|---|
| 949 | May 4, 1873. | C. | Simmons, Lillie Mary | | |
| 950 | " | | Lambert, Frances Clara | | |
| 951 | " | | Bennett, Martha Jane | | |
| 952 | " | | Knowles, Ella Elizabeth | | |
| 953 | " | | Garry, Robert | | |
| 954 | " | | Wright, George Henry | | |
| 955 | " | | Saraw, William McClellan | | |
| 956 | " | | Townsend, Bertram George | * | April 22, 1882 |
| 957 | " | | Townsend, Edward Candee | | |
| 958 | " | | Campbell, Mary Horkuse | | |
| 959 | " | | McRea, Janette Elbertine | | |
| 960 | July 6, 1873. | C. | Baldwin, Clara H. (Crocker) | | |
| 961 | " | | Bradley, Sarah A | | |
| 962 | Sept. 7, 1873. | C. | Rignal, Lydia Edith | | |
| 963 | Oct. 31, 1873. | L. | Burrell, Ellen Louisa | L. | Dec. 15, 1884 |
| 964 | " | | Stahl, Kate Anna | * | April 1, 1880 |
| 965 | Jan. 2, 1874. | L. | Trautman, Peter | L. | May 12, 1878 |
| 966 | " | | Trantman, Catharine A., Mrs | | " |
| 967 | Feb. 27, 1874. | L. | McChesney, George R | G. | Sept. 8, 1882 |
| 968 | " | | McChesney, Anna, Mrs | L. | March 29. 1882 |
| 969 | " | | Manning, Rachel A | L. | Nov. 27, 1878 |
| 970 | " | | Wilson, Helena M., Mrs | | |
| 971 | March 1, 1874. | C. | Keller, Jacob F | G. | June 30, 1882 |
| 972 | " | | Keller, Sarah, Mrs | | |
| 973 | " | | Hawks, Mary Ann, Mrs | * | Feb. 17, 1877 |
| 974 | " | | Hawks. Alfred J | * | Jan. 13, 1883 |
| 975 | May 3, 1874. | C. | Carpenter, Benjamin Charles | L. | May 19, 1879 |
| 976 | " | | Hamlin, Jane | L. | March 2, 1881 |
| 977 | " | | Lawrence, Martha Janette | | |
| 978 | " | | Onderdonk, John Austin | L. | Oct. 20, 1874 |
| 979 | July 5, 1874. | L. | Dickey, John H | | |
| 980 | " | | Dickey, Cornelia | | |
| 981 | " | | Dickey, Frances M. (Richardson) | | |
| 982 | July 3, 1874. | L. | Graves, Edmond F | G. | Jan. 4, 1884 |
| 983 | " | | Graves, Julia B., Mrs E. F | | " |
| 984 | " | | Lambert, Jennie, Mrs | | |
| 985 | Oct. 30, 1874. | L. | Leonard, Jennie | L. | Aug. 13, 1884 |
| 986 | Nov. 1, 1874. | C. | Newton, Lewis | W. | May 11, 1877 |
| 987 | Jan. 3, 1875. | C. | McKee, Dinwoody | L. | Dec. 12, 1883 |
| 988 | " | | McKee, Martha C, Mrs. D | | " |
| 989 | March 7, 1875. | C. | Dudney, Ella Leggett (Garry) | | |
| 990 | " | | Long, Charles | | |
| 991 | " | | McEwen, Maggie B | L. | April 19, 1882 |
| 992 | " | | McGough, Joseph Henry | | |
| 993 | July 2, 1875. | L. | Rushmore, Mary J., Mrs | | |
| 994 | July 4, 1875. | C. | Rushmore, William J | | |
| 995 | July 18, 1875. | L | Burrell, Myron L | | |
| 996 | Sept. 5, 1875. | C. | Newton, Janette T. Mrs | | |
| 997 | Nov. 5, 1875. | L | Lerch, Alice E. (Smith) | | |
| 998 | " | | Stukins, Kittie V. Z., Mrs. Chas | | |
| 999 | Nov. 7, 1875. | C. | Foster, Anna Louisa | L. | Sept. 13, 1876 |
| 1000 | Jan. 6, 1876. | L. | Ballet, Sarah A | | |
| 1001 | " | | Ballet, Lizzle B | | |
| 1002 | March 3, 1876. | L. | Gould John | | |
| 1003 | March 5, 1876. | C. | Noble, John, Jr | | |
| 1004 | " | | Ball, Robert H | L. | Sept. 8, 1882 |
| 1005 | " | | Rebasz, Mary Amanda (Sult) | * | Jan. 23, 1881 |

## MEMBERS OF THE CHURCH (*Continued*).

| NO. | RECEIVED. | | SUBSEQUENT MEMBERS. | REMOVED. | |
|---|---|---|---|---|---|
| 1006 | March 5, 1876. | C. | Bogardus, Ann Mary........ ......... | | |
| 1007 | May 5, 1876. | L. | Daniels, Elizabeth, Mrs............. | | |
| 1008 | May 7, 1876. | C. | Daniels, Ralph William ................ | L. | Nov. 4, 1881 |
| 1009 | July 14, 1876. | L. | Gooding, Stephen F..................... | | |
| 1010 | " | | Gooding, Eliza R..................... | * | May 12, 1884 |
| 1011 | " | | Graves, William H.................... | L. | March 7, 1880 |
| 1012 | Sept. 3, 1876. | C. | Stevens, Lawrence B................... | | |
| 1013 | Jan. 7, 1877. | C. | Spalding, Asa L..................... | | |
| 1014 | " | | Spalding, Isabel, Mrs. A. L........... | | |
| 1015 | " | | Spalding, Frank M.................... | | |
| 1016 | " | | Spalding, Cora I. (Blair)............. | | |
| 1017 | " | | Rose, Bertha A...................... | L. | July 28, 1880 |
| 1018 | " | | Raymond, Orange J................... | * | March 19, 1877 |
| 1019 | " | | Holbrook, Carrie W. (Thompson) ...... | L. | March 14, 1883 |
| 1020 | " | | Holbrook, Anna B. ................... | * | Dec. 20, 1880 |
| 1021 | " | | Holbrook, Esther A., Mrs............. | | |
| 1022 | " | | Brown. Ernestine (Condon) ........... | | |
| 1023 | " | | Warren, Mary E. (McNair) ........... | | |
| 1024 | " | | Keck, Mary A., Mrs.................. | | |
| 1025 | " | | Long. Angeline E. ................... | | |
| 1026 | March 4, 1877. | L. | MacKay, Susannah, Mrs............... | | |
| 1027 | " | | Brackett, Anna Clayton Warren........ | L. | Jan. 30, 1884 |
| 1028 | " | C. | Allen. Sarah Lillian ................. | | |
| 1029 | " | | Cook, Mary Jane, Mrs............. . . | L. | Feb. 27, 1885 |
| 1030 | " | | Daggett, Mary Agnes, Mrs.. ........... | | |
| 1031 | " | | Galliher, Isabel...................... | | |
| 1032 | " | | Green, Eglantine Hemsinger (Laney)... | | |
| 1033 | " | | Higgins. Violetta Maria ............. | | |
| 1034 | " | | Hoag, Florina Adelle (Duff) ......... | | |
| 1035 | " | | Martin, George .. | | |
| 1036 | " | | Martin, Eliza..... . ............... | | |
| 1037 | " | | Mills, James ....................... | W. | Nov. 12, 1884 |
| 1038 | " | | Mills, Mary Jane..................... | * | April 20, 1881 |
| 1039 | " | | Merritt, Mary Jane .................. | | |
| 1040 | " | | Moody, Mary Sophia.................. | | |
| 1041 | " | | Newton. Walter Grant................ | | |
| 1042 | " | | Oliver, Persis.. | | |
| 1043 | " | | Price, Joel D.. ................... | | |
| 1044 | " | | Richardson, Ellsworth M.............. | | |
| 1045 | " | | Sherman, John Henry................. | W. | Oct. 3, 1877 |
| 1046 | " | | Smith, James Bacon................ .... | | |
| 1047 | " | | Tabor, Edward Ransom................ | L. | Jan. 17, 1881 |
| 1048 | " | | Tabor, Eliza S., Mrs................. | | " |
| 1049 | " | | Warren, Jonathan. ............... | | |
| 1050 | " | | Warren, Naomi Douglas .............. | | |
| 1051 | " | | Warren, Mary Elizabeth... ........ | | |
| 1052 | " | | Weaver, Plumilla.................... | | |
| 1053 | " | | Williams, John Stinson .............. | L. | June 23, 1880 |
| 1054 | " | | Williams, Clarabella Jane............. | L. | Jan. 12, 1881 |
| 1055 | " | | Williams, Marian Mahala (Steele)...... | | |
| 1056 | " | | Williams, Henry James............... | L. | Jan. 12, 1881 |
| 1057 | " | | Compton, William Chambers .......... | | |
| 1058 | " | | Compton, Mary Alice, Mrs. ......... | | |
| 1059 | May 6, 1877. | C. | Eberts, Augustina Maria........ . .... | * | Oct. 1, 1877 |
| 1060 | " | | Eberts, Charles Henry................ | | |
| 1061 | " | | Fellows, Eliza ......... ............. | L. | July 30, 1884 |
| 1062 | " | | Fellows, Clarabel.................... | | " |

## MEMBERS OF THE CHURCH (*Continued*).

| NO. | RECEIVED. | SUBSEQUENT MEMBERS. | REMOVED. |
|---|---|---|---|
| 1063 | May 6, 1877. C. | Graves, George Washington............ | L. May 17, 1882 |
| 1064 | " | Graves, Sarah Ellen .................... | " |
| 1065 | " | Haines, Jessie Elizabeth .............. | ................... |
| 1066 | " | Haines, Alice Cantine................. | ................... |
| 1067 | " | James, William ...................... | W. Feb. 18, 1885 |
| 1068 | " | James, Rachel, Mrs... | |
| 1069 | " | Leinbaugh, Ada Mary................. | L. Feb. 12, 1879 |
| 1070 | " | Mayberry, Agnes (Dubay)............. | L. May 14, 1884 |
| 1071 | " | Mayberry, Mary Louise............ .... | * Aug. 25, 1882 |
| 1072 | " | Mayberry, Alice (Taft) ............... | ................... |
| 1073 | " | Smith, Clara Maria.................. | |
| 1074 | " . | Smith, Eugene John................. | G. June 30, 1882 |
| 1075 | " | Wadhams, Amy Spalding (Lerch)...... | ............ |
| 1076 | " L. | Howe, Mary Ette, Mrs............... | |
| 1077 | July 1, 1877. C. | Barnes, Romain A.................. | |
| 1078 | " | Barnes, Mary E..................... | ............ |
| 1079 | " | Geer, Jessie (Puriance)............. | L. July 16, 1882 |
| 1080 | " | Reed, Alice Mary................... | ................... |
| 1081 | " | Robinson, Agnes W................. | |
| 1082 | Nov. 4, 1877. L. | Cady, Flora A. (Eaton).............. | * Dec. 9, 1883 |
| 1083 | " | Maclay, Janette H.................. | ................... |
| 1084 | " C | Casey, Julia....................... | ................... |
| 1085 | " | Casey, Nancy ..................... | ................... |
| 1086 | " | Perry, Carrie, Mrs................. | |
| 1087 | " | Smith, Augusta E., Mrs............. | G. Feb. 14, 1883 |
| 1088 | Feb. 22, 1878. L. | Fillmore, Jared B.................. | L. Oct. 12, 1881 |
| 1089 | " | Fillmore, Emily D........ ......... | " |
| 1090 | Nov. 3, 1878. L. | Tinker, Ezra, Rev................. | L. Jan. 25, 1879 |
| 1091 | " | Tinker, Mary Jannette............. | " |
| 1092 | " C. | Clark, Helen M.................... | ................... |
| 1093 | " | Clark, Frances E.................. | ................... |
| 1094 | " | Chubbuck, Elijah.................. | * March 6, 1884 |
| 1095 | " | Chubbuck, Harriet, Mrs. E.......... | L. June 4, 1884 |
| 1096 | " | Howd, Eleanor, Mrs................ | ................... |
| 1097 | " | Mudd, Fawn.. .................... | ................... |
| 1098 | " | Mudd, Mary Ann. | ................... |
| 1099 | " | Wayman, Sarah (Fogleson).......... | L. Feb. 22, 1882 |
| 1100 | Jan. 5, 1879. L. | Whedan, Cornelia, Mrs...... | ................... |
| 1101 | " | Woodward, Sarah, Mrs............. | |
| 1102 | " | Clark, Eliza E., Mrs.............. | ................... |
| 1103 | " C. | Dandler, Jules George.... | |
| 1104 | March 2, 1879. C. | Beach, Jennie M.............. | |
| 1105 | " | Campbell, Chloe Maria............. | |
| 1106 | " | Campbell, Florence Alvira......... | ............ |
| 1107 | " | Crocker, Edwin Augustus.......... | |
| 1108 | " | Crocker, Homer................... | |
| 1109 | " | Folger, Louisa, Mrs............... | |
| 1110 | " | Hoag, William Cushman.... . ...... | L. Nov. 30, 1881 |
| 1111 | " | Jones, Loraine................... | |
| 1112 | " | Fellows, Fred Ephraim.... ... | ............ |
| 1113 | " | Kinney, Cora (Taylor)............. | ................... |
| 1114 | " | Kinney, Lydia Annetta........... | ................... |
| 1115 | " | LeValley, Augusta .... | |
| 1116 | " | McRae, Isabel.................... | |
| 1117 | " | Mackey, Rosetta Sophia (Lee)....... | ................... |
| 1118 | " | Merritt, Louis ................... | |
| 1119 | " | Nelles, Anna...................... | L. Dec. 26, 1883 |

5

## 98

### MEMBERS OF THE CHURCH (*Continued*).

| NO. | RECEIVED. | | SUBSEQUENT MEMBERS. | REMOVAL. |
|---|---|---|---|---|
| 1120 | March 2, 1879. | C. | Sleeper. George | |
| 1121 | " | | Scott, Edward William. | |
| 1122 | " | | Scott, Walter Elisha | |
| 1123 | " | | Townsend, Elmer B. | |
| 1124 | " | | Van Vleet, Eliza B., Mrs. | |
| 1125 | " | | Van Vleet, Ada Estelle | * May 23, 1885 |
| 1126 | " | | Wright, Frank Ellsworth. | |
| 1127 | " | | Woodward, Sarah Alletta (McComb) | |
| 1128 | " | | Woodward, Eliza Davis | |
| 1129 | " | | Woodward, Milton | |
| 1130 | May 11, 1879. | C. | Van Wagoner, Susie | |
| 1131 | Oct. 22, 1879. | L. | Furbish, Edward Brown | |
| 1132 | Nov. 7, 1879. | L. | Furbish, Grace H. T. | |
| 1133 | " | | Furbish, Elizabeth Harrison | * Feb. 24, 1884 |
| 1134 | " | | King Maria L., Mrs. | |
| 1135 | Jan. 2, 1880. | L. | Gatchell, Cynthia | |
| 1136 | " | | Kelsey, Helen J. | |
| 1137 | March 5, 1880. | L | Ives, Frances E. | |
| 1138 | " | | Wright, Ida M | |
| 1139 | April 30, 1880. | L. | Morris, Margaret | L. Nov. 21, 1883 |
| 1140 | May 2, 1880. | C. | Gilbert, Jane. | |
| 1141 | July 11, 1860. | C. | Gardner, Salome | |
| 1142 | " | | Mulholland, Eliza A., Mrs. | |
| 1143 | " | | Mulholland, James S. | |
| 1144 | Sept. 5, 1880. | C. | Hamilton, Robert. | |
| 1145 | " | | Hamilton, Margaret. | |
| 1146 | Nov. 7, 1880. | C. | Day, Mary, Mrs | |
| 1147 | " | | Dietrick, Lyman A. | |
| 1148 | " | | Dietrick, Emma | |
| 1149 | March 6, 1881. | C. | Bennett, Agnes Elizabeth | |
| 1150 | " | | Furbish, Clinton Hart. | |
| 1151 | " | | Lerch, Arthur Leonard. | |
| 1152 | May 1, 1881. | L. | Pomeroy, Daniel | |
| 1153 | " | | Pomeroy, Harriet Elizabeth | |
| 1154 | " | C. | Duncan, Robert Wallace | |
| 1155 | " | | Duncan, Clarissa Agnes. | |
| 1156 | " | | Nichols, Lillian Evangeline (Smith) | |
| 1157 | July 3, 1881. | L. | Baker, Flavius J. | |
| 1158 | " | | Baker, Isa B | |
| 1159 | " | | Baker, Flavia Edith. | |
| 1160 | " | C. | Gilbert, Herbert. | |
| 1161 | " | | Washburn, Fred Enoch. | |
| 1162 | " | | Washburn, Charles Armstrong | |
| 1163 | Sept. 4, 1881. | L. | Haskell, Martin N. | |
| 1164 | " | | Haskell, Cornelia L | |
| 1165 | Nov. 6, 1881. | L. | Marshall, Fredreka | |
| 1166 | " | | Flagler, Sarah. | |
| 1167 | " | C. | Steele, Amelia | L. July 30, 1884 |
| 1168 | " | | Chappell, Ellen, Mrs | |
| 1169 | " | | Chappell, Ellen J. M | |
| 1170 | Jan. 1, 1882. | L. | Baker, Thaddeus. | |
| 1171 | " | | Baker, Sarah. | |
| 1172 | July 2, 1882. | C. | Reynolds, Josephine | |
| 1173 | " | L. | Jenkins, William J. | |
| 1174 | " | | Rose, Elizabeth L. | |
| 1175 | " | | Rose, Bertha A. | |
| 1176 | March 4, 1883. | C. | Aldrich, Mary (Boughton) | |

## MEMBERS OF THE CHURCH (*Continued*).

| NO. | RECEIVED. | | SUBSEQUENT MEMBERS. | REMOVED. |
|---|---|---|---|---|
| 1177 | March 4, 1883. | C. | Clark, Mattie (Gascoyne)............... | ................... |
| 1178 | " | | Jennings, George..................... | ................... |
| 1179 | " | | Reed, May......................... | ................... |
| 1180 | " | | Webster, Addie Julia................. | ................. |
| 1181 | May 6, 1883. | L. | Day, Hattie M...................... | .... ........... |
| 1182 | " | C. | Day, George ...................... | ................... |
| 1183 | July 1, 1883. | L. | Scott, Mary, Mrs.................... | ................... |
| 1184 | " | | Scott, Luella...................... | ................... |
| 1185 | Sept. 2, 1883. | L. | Allen, Thomas A .................... | ................... |
| 1186 | " | / | Allen, Minnie...................... | ................... |
| 1187 | Nov. 4, 1883. | L. | Manning, Mary A .................... | ................... |
| 1188 | " | | Kent, Walter F..................... | ................... |
| 1189 | " | | Kent, Ella A ...................... | ................... |
| 1190 | " | | Saraw, Mary P...................... | ................... |
| 1191 | " | | Moore, Alexander................... | ................... |
| 1192 | June 6, 1884. | L. | Odell, Rachel ..................... | ................. |
| 1193 | Jan. 6, 1884. | C. | Ward, Cleland A.................... | ................... |
| 1194 | Mar. 16, 1884. | C. | Baker, Sarah Agnes.................. | ................... |
| 1195 | " | | Ball, Tom Lawrence.................. | ................... |
| 1196 | " | | Bogardus, Carrie Elizabeth............ | ................... |
| 1197 | " | | Burnette, Morris S.................. | ................... |
| 1198 | " | | Clark, Sarah Lucy................... | ................... |
| 1199 | " | | Clark, Annie L. D.................. | ................... |
| 1200 | " | | Compton, Harry Alfred............... | ................... |
| 1201 | " | | Cornelius, Annie ................... | ................... |
| 1202 | " | | Crosby, Grace Mary.................. | ................... |
| 1203 | " | | Dickey, Hattie Florence.............. | ................... |
| 1204 | " | | Dickinson, Hattie................... | ................... |
| 1205 | " | | Dietrick, Will Arthur................ | ................... |
| 1206 | " | | Dietrick, Lester Angelo.............. | ................... |
| 1207 | " | | Emery, Mary, Mrs................... | .... .. |
| 1208 | " | | Fisher, Frances S .................. | ................... |
| 1209 | " | | Fisher, Grace M ................... | .. ..... |
| 1210 | " | | Fitts, Ada May..................... | ................... |
| 1211 | " | | Fitts, Florence..................... | ................... |
| 1212 | " | | Furbish, Robert Townsend............. | ................... |
| 1213 | " | | Gantt, Emiline Flagler (Foote)......... | ................... |
| 1214 | " | | Gantt, Mary M..................... | ................... |
| 1215 | " | | Gardner, Ella F ................... | ................... |
| 1216 | " | | Graham, Emma Mabel................ | .. ......... |
| 1217 | " | | Graham, Mary Jane.................. | ................... |
| 1218 | " | | Graham, Virgil...... | ................... |
| 1219 | " | | Gunn, Maggie T.................... | ................... |
| 1220 | " | | Hamilton, Margaret Isadora........... | ................... |
| 1221 | " | | Haskell, Amy Ann................... | ................... |
| 1222 | " | L. | Haskell, Phineas N.................. | ................... |
| 1223 | " | C. | Hendershot, Fanny May.............. | ................... |
| 1224 | " | | Holbrook, Grace Mary ............... | ................... |
| 1225 | " | | King, Frank....................... | ................... |
| 1226 | " | | Klingensmith, Nettie Isabel........... | ................... |
| 1227 | " | | Longtoft, Emma, Mrs................ | ... ...... |
| 1228 | " | | Leller, Louis ...................... | ................... |
| 1229 | " | | Lerch, Mary Eugenia................ | ................... |
| 1230 | " | | Lerch, William Baltz................ | ................... |
| 1231 | " | | LeValley, Gertrude E................ | ................... |
| 1232 | " | | Merritt, Mary Eloise................ | ................... |
| 1233 | " | | Mix, Nora Alice... .................. | ................... |

## MEMBERS OF THE CHURCH (*Continued*).

| NO. | RECEIVED. | | SUBSEQUENT MEMBERS. | REMOVED. | |
|---|---|---|---|---|---|
| 1234 | Mch. 16, 1884. | C. | Moody, Nettie C | | |
| 1235 | " | | Morrill, Austin D | | |
| 1236 | " | | Murray, Isabel Cady | | |
| 1237 | " | | Parker, Tryphena M | * Jan. | 23, 1885 |
| 1238 | " | | Perry, Mary Minerva | | |
| 1239 | " | | Prime, John A | | |
| 1240 | " | | Pomeroy, Nora Lavinia | * May | 23, 1885 |
| 1241 | " | | Richardson, Charles | | |
| 1242 | " | | Richardson, Alice | | |
| 1243 | " | | Rose, Ernest Lou. | | |
| 1244 | " | | Spalding, Grace Ethel | | |
| 1245 | " | | Steele, Ebbie May | L. July | 30, 1884 |
| 1246 | " | | Stevens, Cynthia | L. July | 9, 1884 |
| 1247 | " | | Stevens, Mary Ellen | " | |
| 1248 | " | | Trankle, Fred | | |
| 1249 | " | | Trevor, Caroline May | | |
| 1250 | " | | Ticknor, Elizabeth | | |
| 1251 | " | | Ticknor, Grace | | |
| 1252 | " | | Timmerman, Walter Thomas | | |
| 1253 | " | | Watson, Mary Jane | | |
| 1254 | " | | Watson, Olive Maud | | |
| 1255 | " | | Webster, Grace Elizabeth | | |
| 1256 | " | | Windsor, George | | |
| 1257 | " | | Windsor, William, Jr | | |
| 1258 | " | | Woolworth, Eugene | | |
| 1259 | " | L. | Wilson, Mary M., Mrs | | |
| 1260 | May 4, 1884. | C. | Babcock, Mary Elizabeth | | |
| 1261 | " | | Creamer, Caroline, Mrs. | | |
| 1262 | " | | Ellis, Henry A | | |
| 1263 | " | | Ellis, Susie Evangeline | | |
| 1264 | " | | Folger, Hattie Elizabeth | | |
| 1265 | " | | Knoop, George | | |
| 1266 | " | | McRae, Frances Elbertine | | |
| 1267 | " | | McRae, Agnes Elbertine | | |
| 1268 | " | | Moss, Laura | | |
| 1269 | " | | Nottleman, William J | | |
| 1270 | " | | Reynolds, Mabel | | |
| 1271 | " | | Scott, Robert | | |
| 1272 | " | | Scott, Jessie | | |
| 1273 | " | | Weaver, Minnie E | | |
| 1274 | July 6, 1884. | C. | Westcott, Samantha, Mrs | | |
| 1275 | " | | Clark, George E | | |
| 1276 | July 13, 1884. | C. | Wakeman, Helen Edna | | |
| 1277 | " | | Beach, Mary Cyrene | | |
| 1278 | " | L. | Murray, Mary P. | | |
| 1279 | May 1, 1885. | L. | Ferguson, Sarah M. | | |
| 1280 | May 5, 1885. | C. | Campbell, Alice | | |

# Alphabetical Index.

| No. | Name. | No. | Name. |
|---|---|---|---|
| 1077 | Barnes. Romaine A. | 243 | Boardman. Edwin L. |
| 159 | Barnes, Sophronia | 279 | Boardman. Henry |
| 909 | Barney. Jennie E. W. | 40 | Boardman, Lucretia A. |
| 468 | Barr. Gabriel | 288 | Boardman, Lucy J. |
| 330 | Barrett. Sophia | 244 | Boardman. William F. |
| 704 | Batten. Charles D. | 617 | Bowman. Ernestine |
| 854 | Bayley, Almira | 849 | Bowman. Mary |
| 1004 | Beach. Jennie M. | 78 | Bowne. Mary E. |
| 1277 | Beach. Mary Cyrene | 1006 | Bogardus. Ann Mary |
| 877 | Bedford. Eliza | 879 | Bogardus, Caroline |
| 791 | Bedford. Mary J. | 1196 | Bogardus, Carrie E. |
| 160 | Beebe. Demmiz | 800 | Bogardus, Charles E. |
| 171 | Beebe. John | 1027 | Brackett, Anna C. |
| 191 | Beebe, Julia | 961 | Bradley, Sarah A. |
| 175 | Beebe. Lucinda M. | 88 | Bramin. Nancy |
| 490 | Belden, Angeline G. | 240 | Bratt. Laura |
| 161 | Belden, Henry | 469 | Brazee. Mary C. |
| 59 | Belden. Mary A. | 682 | Briggs, Mary L. |
| 239 | Belden. Melissa | 661 | Brink. Delia |
| 58 | Belden. Reuben C. | 810 | Brink, Elvira H. |
| 1149 | Bennett. Agnes Isabel | 635 | Brink. Melissa J. |
| 816 | Bennett. Alice | 92 | Brock. Loretta [peace. |
| 712 | Bennett. Edwin M. | 651 | Broderick. Delilah Make- |
| 462 | Bennett. Eliza A. | 120 | Bronson. Noah L. |
| 340 | Bennett, Frances E. | 121 | Bronson. Sophia |
| 919 | Bennett. John C. | 672 | Brown, Almeda F. |
| 461 | Bennett. Joseph L. | 396 | Brown, Betsey R. |
| 713 | Bennett. Julia A. | 736 | Brown, Charles C. |
| 951 | Bennett. Martha Jane | 553 | Brown. Denison D. |
| 135 | Bentley, Joseph | 402 | Brown. Eliza |
| 805 | Benton. Lucy | 479 | Brown, Eliza |
| 136 | Bird. Ann D. | 1022 | Brown, Ernestine |
| 613 | Birdsall. Harriet | 555 | Brown. Harriet |
| 944 | Bissell Frances A. (Reed) | 272 | Brown, John G. |
| 488 | Biter. Barbara | 401 | Brown, Levi |
| 1016 | Blair. Cora Spalding | 273 | Brown, Lucy |
| 830 | Blair, George | 941 | Brown, Minnie Frances |
| 612 | Blair, Mary | 737 | Brown, Maria R. |
| 662 | Blair. Mary A. | 214 | Brown. Samuel B. |
| 631 | Blair. William | 449 | Brown. Samuel B. |
| 466 | Blackley, Richard | 554 | Brown. Sarah |
| 467 | Blackley. Susan | 474 | Brown. L. Aurelia |
| 123 | Blinn. Clarissa | 52 | Brown. Sophrona |
| 514 | Blinn. Frances E. | 450 | Brown. Sophronia S. |
| 389 | Bloomfield. Mary E. | 410 | Brown. Sylinda |

# 103

104

ALPHABETICAL INDEX (*Continued*).

| No. | Name. | No. | Name. |
|---|---|---|---|
| 385 | Cole, Cornelius S. | 67 | Crocker, Luther, Jr. |
| 392 | Cole, Philetta E. | 720 | Crocker, Martha S. |
| 246 | Cole William E. | 471 | Crocker, Orpha E. |
| 513 | Collier, Mary E. | 704 | Crocker, Robert |
| 624 | Colt, Sarah E. | 28 | Crocker, Sarah |
| 290 | Colton, Jane H. | 359 | Crocker, Sarah M. |
| 1200 | Compton, Harry Alfred | 855 | Crocker, Sarah G. |
| 1058 | Compton, Mary Alice | 96 | Crosby, Aaron |
| 1057 | Compton, Wm. Chambers | 206 | Crosby, Gabriella |
| 264 | Condon, Amelia | 1202 | Crosby, Grace Mary |
| 1022 | Condon, Ernestine | 91 | Crumb, Elizabeth |
| 379 | Connett, George W. | 883 | Culver, Isaac C. |
| 591 | Cook, Hiram A. | 295 | Curry, Mary Ann |
| 592 | Cook, Lucinda | 260 | Curry, Minerva |
| 1029 | Cook, Mary Jane | 275 | Curtis, Apphia |
| 727 | Cooley, Elizabeth | 432 | Curtis, Esther A. |
| 728 | Cooley, Emma | 516 | Curtis, Phebe A. |
| 895 | Cooper, Ellen H. | 274 | Curtis, Worthy |
| 894 | Cooper, James W. | 588 | Curtis, Sarah S. |
| 131 | Corbin, Mary F. | | |
| 223 | Corbin, Phebe M. | 1030 | Daggett, Mary Agnes |
| 1201 | Cornelius, Annie | 532 | Daly, Mrs. |
| 846 | Craig, Joseph | 1103 | Dandler, Jules George |
| 753 | Crampton, Almira W. | 1007 | Daniels, Elizabeth |
| 752 | Crampton, Hesekiah R. | 509 | Daniels, Lucy |
| 646 | Crapsey, Addie | 1008 | Daniels, Ralph William |
| 813 | Crapsey, Florence L. | 242 | Davenport, Ada H. |
| 719 | Crapsey, George | 277 | Davenport, Clarissa |
| 645 | Crapsey, Jane | 276 | Davenport, Darius |
| 720 | Crapsey, Martha S. | 251 | Davenport, Eliza J. |
| 676 | Craw, Alanson | 520 | Davidson, Sarah Jane |
| 1261 | Creamer, Caroline | 110 | Davis, Cynthia |
| 614 | Crocker, Alice E. | 347 | Davis, Edward W. |
| 414 | Crocker, Charles A. | 1182 | Day, George |
| 960 | Crocker, Clara H. | 1181 | Day, Hattie M. |
| 161 | Crocker, Cornelia M. | 458 | Day, Marian W. |
| 470 | Crocker, Daniel P. | 1146 | Day, Mary |
| 1107 | Crocker, Edwin A. | 930 | Day, William |
| 719 | Crocker, George | 299 | Dempsey, Frances |
| 26 | Crocker, Hannah | 924 | Dennis, Eliza |
| 481 | Crocker, Hannah S. | 509 | Depew, Lucy |
| 1108 | Crocker, Homer | 1148 | Dietrick, Emma |
| 480 | Crocker, J. Newton | 1206 | Dietrick, Lester Angelo |
| 27 | Crocker, Josiah | 1147 | Dietrick, Lyman A. |
| 25 | Crocker, Luther | 1205 | Dietrick, Will Arthur |

## 105

ALPHABETICAL INDEX (*Continued*).

| No. | NAME. | No. | NAME. |
|---|---|---|---|
| 868 | Dick, Mary | 478 | Dunton, Austin |
| 876 | Dick, Nicholas | 519 | Dunton, Helen M. |
| 980 | Dickey, Cornelia | 196 | Duquet, Joseph |
| 981 | Dickey, Frances M. | 218 | Duquet, Mary |
| 1203 | Dickey, Hattie Florence | 794 | Duquet, Mary J. |
| 979 | Dickey, John H. | 795 | Duquet, Sarah J. |
| 1204 | Dickinson, Hattie | 345 | Durfie, Jamuel G. |
| 232 | Dickinson, Israel | 300 | Earl, Mary |
| 234 | Dickinson, Israel G. | 1082 | Eaton, Flora A. |
| 233 | Dickinson, Polly | 1059 | Eberts, Augustina Maria |
| 286 | Dickinson, Sophia | 1060 | Eberts, Charles Henry |
| 525 | Dill, Catharine B. | 1207 | Emery, Mary |
| 511 | Dill, Deborah | 1262 | Ellis, Henry A. |
| 435 | Dill, Elizabeth | 1263 | Ellis, Susie Evangeline |
| 651 | Dingman, Delilah | 797 | Eshbach, Annie M. |
| 567 | Dingman, Catharine | 582 | Evans, Agnes W. |
| 746 | Dingman, George G. | 354 | Evans, Lucinda |
| 745 | Dingman, George W. | | |
| 283 | Donnelly, Dudley | 673 | Farwell, Ella |
| 765 | Dornen, John | 108 | Farley, Maria L. |
| 444 | Doty, Mary J. | 1062 | Fellows, Clarabel |
| 66 | Doud, Eleanor | 1061 | Fellows, Eliza |
| 89 | Doud, Eunice | 1109 | Fellows, Fred E. |
| 117 | Doud, Lophonzo | 672 | Ferguson, Almeda |
| 137 | Doud, Lorenzo | 407 | Ferguson, Ann |
| 92 | Doud, Loretta | 406 | Ferguson, James |
| 90 | Doud, Vesta Ann | 671 | Ferguson, Mary |
| 793 | Drake, Frances M. | 681 | Ferguson, Sarah |
| 835 | Drake, George | 1279 | Ferguson, Sarah M. |
| 1070 | Dubay, Agnes | 875 | Fiddler, Margaret |
| 259 | Dudley, Theodore O. | 874 | Fiddler, Rush |
| 989 | Dudney, Ella Leggette | 1089 | Fillmore, Emily D. |
| 812 | Dumville, Eliza J., Mackey | 1088 | Fillmore, Jared B. |
| 1155 | Duncan, Clarissa Agnes | 770 | Finn, Albert |
| 673 | Duncan, Ella F. | 678 | Finn, Elizabeth |
| 422 | Duncan, Frances | 607 | Finn, Jane T. |
| 1154 | Duncan, Robert Wallace | 334 | Fisher, Cornelia C. |
| 1034 | Duff, Florina Addie | 1208 | Fisher, Frances S. |
| 859 | Dunkelburg, Charles | 1209 | Fisher, Grace M. |
| 83 | Dunn, David R. | 487 | Fitch, Hannah |
| 494 | Dunn, Frances E. | 1210 | Fitts, Ada May |
| 22 | Dunn, Laura W. | 1211 | Fitts, Florence |
| 608 | Dunning, Elizabeth | 625 | Fitts, Harriet G. |
| 828 | Dunning, Samuel | 703 | Fitts, James F. |
| 811 | Dunton, Addie L. | 113 | Fitzgerald, Ann Eliza |

ALPHABETICAL INDEX (*Continued*).

ALPHABETICAL INDEX (*Continued*).

| No. | NAME. | No. | NAME. |
|---|---|---|---|
| 787 | McMaster, James M. | 612 | Morrel, Mary Blair |
| 786 | McMaster, Mary E. | 1139 | Morris, Margaret |
| 304 | McMaster, William | 439 | Morse, Abigail |
| 1023 | McNair, Mary E. | 438 | Morse, Edward |
| 1267 | McRae, Agnes Elbertine | 436 | Morse, James H. |
| 1266 | McRae, Frances Elbertine | 5 | Morse, Joseph C. |
| 1116 | McRae, Isabel | 437 | Morse, Harriet S. |
| 959 | McRae, Janette Elbertine | 86 | Morse, Lydia M. W. |
| 891 | McRae, Sarah | 473 | Morse, Sarah E. |
| 1118 | Merritt, Louis | 97 | Moss, Charles S. |
| 1232 | Merritt, Mary Eloise | 37 | Moss, Harriet M. |
| 1039 | Merritt, Mary Jane | 238 | Moss, Harriet S. |
| 162 | Miles, Martha | 1268 | Moss, Laura |
| 306 | Miller, Lucy | 866 | Moss, Mary E. |
| 69 | Mills, Amelia | 278 | Mott, Chloe |
| 1037 | Mills, James | 912 | Moyer, Frank J. |
| 1038 | Mills, Mary J. | 655 | Moyer, Salome E. |
| 584 | Minard, Amanda | 1097 | Mudd, Fawn |
| 937 | Mix, Maria | 1098 | Mudd, Mary Ann |
| 1233 | Mix, Nora Alice | 1142 | Mulholland, Eliza A. |
| 778 | Moody, Edward | 1143 | Mulholland, James S. |
| 621 | Moody, Ella M. | 416 | Murray, Algina |
| 669 | Moody, Calista L. | 415 | Murray, Daniel R. |
| 386 | Moody, Elisha | 1236 | Murray, Isabel Cady |
| 486 | Moody, Ellen R. (Scott) | 1278 | Murray, Mary P. |
| 747 | Moody, George | 932 | Murray, Martha J. |
| 502 | Moody, George H. | 836 | Musson, Charles |
| 734 | Moody, Laura | | |
| 387 | Moody, Margaret | 933 | Naismith, Sarah A. Lambert |
| 1040 | Moody, Mary Sophia | | |
| 1234 | Moody, Nettie C. | 1119 | Nelles, Anna |
| 1191 | Moore, Alexander | 630 | Nelson, Calvin |
| 483 | Moore, Anna P. | 446 | Nelson, Georgie G. D. |
| 404 | Moore, Benjamin E. | 419 | Nesmith, Mary E. |
| 356 | Moore, Charlotte A. | 179 | Newhall, Daniel |
| 610 | Moore, Emma | 282 | Newhall, Daniel, Jr. |
| 517 | Moore, Libbie H. | 247 | Newhall, Elbridge G. |
| 420 | Moore, Lucia O. | 338 | Newhall, Elbridge G. |
| 405 | Moore, Sarah A. | 181 | Newhall, Franklin |
| 473 | Moore, Sarah E. | 182 | Newhall, Frederick W. |
| 53 | Morgan, Lavinia | 180 | Newhall, Harriet |
| 538 | Morgan, Lavinia | 103 | Newhall, Harriet W. |
| 809 | Mormon, Harriet J. | 408 | Newhall, Lucy E. |
| 1235 | Morrel, Austin D. | 310 | Newhall, Melissa M. |
| 829 | Morrel, Ephraim, K. | 44 | Newhall, Nancy C. |

ALPHABETICAL INDEX (*Continued*).

## 114

# 115

ALPHABETICAL INDEX (*Continued*).

ALPHABETICAL INDEX (*Continued*).

# Members

Received from the organization by letter and confession up to the present time.

| YEAR. | LET. | CON. | TOTAL. | YEAR. | LET. | CON. | TOTAL. |
|-------|------|------|--------|-------|------|------|--------|
| 1838.... | 86 | 6 | 92 | 1862.... | 6 | 3 | 9 |
| 1839.... | 12 | 45 | 57 | 1863.... | 8 | 2 | 10 |
| 1840.... | 65 | 9 | 74 | 1864.... | 9 | ..... | 9 |
| 1841.... | 22 | 33 | 56 | 1865.... | 4 | 2 | 6 |
| 1842.... | 30 | 14 | 44 | 1866.... | 21 | 76 | 97 |
| 1843.. | 13 | 31 | 44 | 1867.... | 5 | 3 | 8 |
| 1844.... | ..... | 1 | 1 | 1868.... | 6 | 10 | 16 |
| 1845.... | 11 | ..... | 11 | 1869.... | 19 | 148 | 167 |
| 1846.... | 10 | ..... | 10 | 1870.... | 5 | 8 | 13 |
| 1847.... | 7 | 2 | 9 | 1871.... | 5 | 4 | 9 |
| 1848.... | 12 | 1 | 13 | 1872.... | 13 | 9 | 22 |
| 1849.... | 9 | 3 | 12 | 1873.... | 4 | 38 | 42 |
| 1850.... | 14 | 10 | 24 | 1874.... | 13 | 9 | 22 |
| 1851.... | 3 | 1 | 4 | 1875.... | 4 | 9 | 13 |
| 1852.... | 5 | 12 | 17 | 1876.... | 7 | 6 | 13 |
| 1853.... | 8 | 4 | 12 | 1877.... | 5 | 70 | 75 |
| 1854.... | 5 | 2 | 7 | 1878.... | 4 | 8 | 12 |
| 1855... | 11 | 3 | 14 | 1879.... | 4 | 27 | 31 |
| 1856.... | 5 | 1 | 6 | 1880.... | 7 | 7 | 14 |
| 1857.... | 4 | ..... | 4 | 1881.... | 9 | 12 | 21 |
| 1858.... | 10 | 61 | 71 | 1882.... | 5 | 1 | 6 |
| 1859.... | 4 | 1 | 5 | 1883.... | 10 | 6 | 16 |
| 1860.... | 11 | 2 | 13 | 1884.... | 4 | 83 | 87 |
| 1861.... | 2 | 1 | 3 | 1885.... | ..... | ..... | ..... |

# CORPORATE NAME

# General Laws of Incorporation.

---

## CORPORATE NAME.

The name of this society is, "The Society of the First Free Congregational Church of Lockport."

## ANNUAL MEETING.

The annual meeting for the election of officers, hearing of reports and the transaction of other appropriate business shall be held at the chapel at two o'clock P. M., on the first Tuesday in December of each year.

## GENERAL LAWS OF INCORPORATION.

1. It shall be lawful for the persons of full age belonging to any church congregation or religious society, other than the Episcopalian and Reformed churches (otherwise provided for), and not already incorporated, to assemble at the place where they statedly worship, and by a plurality of voices elect not less than three nor more than nine discreet persons of their society trustees, to take charge of the estate and property belonging thereto, and to transact all affairs relative to the temporalities thereof; and at such election every person of full age, who has statedly worshiped with such church, congregation or society, and has formerly been considered as belonging thereto, shall be entitled to vote.

2. The said election shall be conducted as follows : The minister, or in his absence an elder or deacon, or if no such officers are pres-

ent then any other person being a member or stated hearer in such church shall publicly notify the congregation of the time when and the place where the said election shall be held, at least fifteen days before the election, such notification being given on two successive Sabbaths preceding the day of election. At the election two elders. or church wardens, or if there be no such officers then two members of the society, to be nominated by a majority, shall preside, receive the votes of electors, be judges of the qualifications of electors, and the officers to return the names of those chosen trustees by a plurality of votes ; and the said returning officers shall immediately thereafter certify under their hands and seals the names of the persons elected trustees, in which certificate the title by which such trustees and their successors shall forever thereafter be known shall be particularly described, which certificate being proved or acknowledged shall be recorded ; and such trustees and their successors shall thereupon be a body corporate by the name or title expressed in such certificate.

3. Certificates of incorporation may be acknowledged before any officer authorized to take acknowledgments of deeds.

4. Any religious society organized under the laws of this state may receive by bequest or devise real or personal estate whose net annual income shall not exceed $12.000 ; provided, if such bequests are from any person who, having a husband, wife, child or parent, gives to benevolent objects more than half of his estate, the entire benevolent bequests are valid to the extent only of one-half the estate.

#### SETTLEMENT AND DISMISSION OF PASTORS.

As to qualifications, investiture of office and spiritual duties of pastors, the civil law has no concern — churches are sole judges. In the settlement, pecuniary support and dismissal of a pastor the law requires, in every incorporated society, that each member of the congregation (being a legal voter) has an equal voice. Individuals may be church members, but if contributing nothing to the support of the society they are not voters in the corporation ; while individuals, even excluded from the church for moral delinquencies, so long as they statedly attend its public services and contribute to the maintenance of the society are corporate legal voters.

## TRUSTEES' ELECTION AND TENURE OF OFFICE.

1. Trustees are to be elected for three years. Immediately after their first election, in any church or society, they shall be divided by lot (as near as may be in equal numbers) into three classes. The seats of the first class shall be vacated at the end of the first year, those of the second class at the end of the second year, and the third class at the expiration of the third year. At least one month before the close of any official term, the trustees shall notify, in writing, the minister, or in case of his death or absence the deacons shall notify the congregation of such fact, specifying the names of the trustees whose terms will expire, when a new election to fill such vacancies which election shall be held, at least six days before such vacancies occur, as hereinbefore provided. All elections, after the first, shall be held and conducted by the same persons and in the same manner as the first, and the result thereof certified by them, and such certificate shall entitle the persons elected to act as trustees.

2. It is the duty of the officers of the society to comply strictly with the requirements of the statute as to the formalities of election. Irregularities in the notice do not, however, necessarily vitiate the result. If due and regular notice is given of a meeting of the society, those present, according to the notice, constitute a quorum, although they may not be a majority of the whole body.

3. No persons are entitled to vote for trustees (after the first election in any church or society) except such as have been stated attendants on divine worship in the church at least one year next preceding, and have contributed to the support of said church or congregation according to the usages and customs thereof. Women of full age, as well as men, are legal voters in the election of trustees. The society clerk is also required to keep a register of the names of all such persons as desire to become stated hearers of said church or society.

4. To entitle a person to vote at any election held by a religious corporation: 1. He must have been for a year a regular attendant

in his own person upon divine worship in the society. 2. He must have contributed substantial and material support, either in money or property, or in service such as is usually paid for, and which he rendered under an agreement that it was to be received in lieu of a pecuniary contributton. Attendance of members of one's family is not such attendance as will satisfy the statute; nor is taking part in the exercises of the society a sufficient contribution to its support.

5. The qualification prescribed by the statute of incorporation for the election of trustees of the society cannot be abridged or extended by any act of the trustees or of the corporators. Every person qualified under the statute has an incontestable right to vote at the election for trustees.

6. If a religious society fails to choose any of the three classes of trustees as provided by statute, such corporation shall not be thereby dissolved, but the trustees already chosen shall continue to hold office until others are elected in their stead; and when such neglect or omission shall happen the trustees of said society shall immediately thereafter give notice, in writing, to the minister, or in case of his death or absence to the deacons, who shall notify the congregation of such omission and appoint the time and place for the election of new trustees, the same order being observed as hereinbefore provided.

7. Whenever a trustee ceases to be a member of such church congregation or society by removal or otherwise, or ceases to statedly attend and support its services, he shall at the same time and for such cause cease to act as trustee, and his place shall be declared vacant by an official notice of the board to the society, and a new election ordered.

8. And when trustees manifest a disposition incompatible with their duties as trustees by acts hostile to the church, they must be considered as having seceded, and, in effect, abdicated their offices, and an injunction will be granted restraining their action as trustees.

#### POWERS AND DUTIES AS TRUSTEES.

1. The great and paramount duty of trustees of religious corporations is to see that the temporalities committed to their charge are

fairly and fully devoted to the purposes the founders had in view. All authority conferred upon them is necessarily subordinate to this end, and all exercise of it beyond the legitimate attainment of this end is usurpation.

2. A religious corporation consists not of the trustees, but of every member of the corporation entitled to vote. Although called the trustees, they do not hold the property individually in trust. It belongs to the society. The trustees, however, are trustees in the strictest sense of responsibility for the property committed to their care, and cannot deal with it for their own benefit.

3. Trustees of a religious corporation can only bind the corporate body by their action at a meeting of the board. Separate action of the trustees, though a majority in number, creates no corporate liability.

4. Trustees of every congregation or society and their successors shall have and use a common seal, and may renew and alter the same at pleasure.

5. The trustees shall administer the temporalities and hold and apply the property and revenues for the benefit of the corporation, according to the discipline, rules and usages of the denomination to which the church members of the corporation belong. And it shall not be lawful to divert such estate, property or revenue to any purposes except the support and maintenance of a church or religious or benevolent institution or object connected with the church or denomination to which such corporation belongs

# Questions for Self-Examination.

1. Do I more carefully observe my engagements with my Saviour in secret prayer than any other appointments? Is it a delight to be alone with him?

2. Do I keep in mind my covenant with my Lord and his with me, in order that I may be faithful to my vows, and as becomes those who are resolved to keep the promises made?

3. Do I *study* the Bible? Do I understand and prize, above all price, its glorious doctrines? Do its precepts regulate my intercourse with men, and my communion with God?

4. How do I spend the Sabbath? Is it to me a day holy to the Lord and honorable? How much of its time do I waste in indolence? How much to dress? How much with God? How much to my soul?

5. What proportion of my worldly property do I sanctify to the Lord? In what do I deny myself for the purpose of doing good?

(124)

6. Do I, in dependence on the Holy Spirit, govern my temper, subdue my passions, and quell a spirit of complaining of those around me, and of fault-finding with my brethren? Am I more willing to pray for and speak to one in error than to mention his sin to a third person?

7. Am I interested in maintaining the services of God's house — in the Sabbath-school, the weekly meetings, the monthly concert? Do I sustain them by my presence, my influence and my heavenly-mindedness?

8. Is my zeal *periodical,* or *constant?* Am I as willing to serve my Saviour when few serve him, as when many serve him? Is there *one* to whom I am *faithful,* and for whose conversion I feel intense anxiety?

9. Do I live as though I was *bought* with *blood,* and had given myself to Jesus Christ? Is it my prayer, in sickness or health, joy or sorrow, life or death, *Thy will, O God, be done?*

# Contents.

www.ingramcontent.com/pod-product-compliance
Lightning Source LLC
Chambersburg PA
CBHW030615270326
41927CB00007B/1186